Craft-
based
Design

Mit Arbeiten von / with works of: Martin Aigner / Peter Bruckner /
Robert Comploj / Rudolf Gritsch / Sandra Haischberger /
Beate von Harten / Arnold Meusburger / Veronika Persché /
Thomas Rösler / Martina Zwölfer | Text: Janko Ferk
Photos / Fotografien: Nikolaus Korab

Craft-based Design

Stefan Moritsch (Ed./Hg.)

On Practical Knowledge
and Manual Creativity /

Von Handwerkern
und Gestaltern

NEW DESIGN
UNIVERSITY

niggli

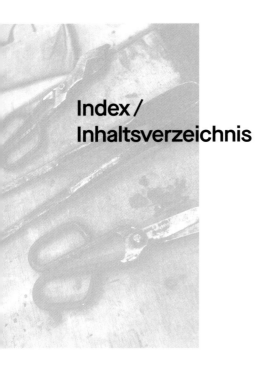

Index /
Inhaltsverzeichnis

Foreword /
Vorwort

Herbert Grüner
Rector of New Design University St. Pölten, Austria /
Rektor der New Design University St. Pölten, Österreich

It is the aim of New Design University (NDU), a private university located in St. Pölten, to address topics belonging to its core subject of design, and to open up connections to related fields in business and technology as well. A young, creative university, the NDU is a place for innovative ideas in education that are grounded scholastically and artistically and linked to relevant professional practice. This is also the reason that, in 2013, our university introduced a course of study that to this day remains unique: Manual & Material Culture.

Through this program, another special feature of the NDU is brought to the foreground, namely regional issues: The university collects, analyzes, and finds solutions for regional matters on an international level. The NDU's approach is also reflected in the portraits of the individuals found in this publication: people working in the region who have international experience and contacts. They make it clear that regional work must never be confused with provincial thinking!

In the same way that regionalism should not be confused with provincialism, "manual crafts" cannot be equated with work that is standardized and exclusively committed to tradition. This publication demonstrates well that, in the 21st century, the manual craft industry has a special opportunity to take advantage of its inherent qualities, such as its autonomous, self-directed work, relying on valid methods and instruments. This is joined by the curiosity of the researcher to turn to current, often very complex problems in a solution-driven approach. And with that, a sense of social responsibility for all that is connected to it. The authors and the portraits of the craftspeople in this publication give expression to this approach, and show how it can be implemented in research, study, and teaching, as well as in the craft industry.

As the rector of the NDU, I would like to thank all those responsible for bringing about this visionary publication. It matches the direction our university is taking in this area of our curriculum, which we consider to be visionary: the research and development of craft methods and methodologies, and the use of the results for manual craft practice and further scholarly and creative explorations in this field.

Es ist der Anspruch der New Design University Privatuniversität St. Pölten (NDU), Themen zu besetzen, die einerseits zu ihrem Kernbereich der Gestaltung zählen, andererseits jedoch auch Zugänge zu angrenzenden Bereichen der Wirtschaft und Technik eröffnen. Damit ist die NDU als junge, kreative Universität ein Ort für innovative Ausbildungskonzepte, die wissenschaftlich beziehungsweise künstlerisch fundiert sind und einen Bezug zur relevanten Praxis aufweisen. Das ist auch der Grund, warum unsere Universität 2013 das bisher einzigartige Studium eingeführt hat: den Studiengang Design, Handwerk & materielle Kultur – Manual & Material Culture.

Nicht zuletzt durch diesen Studiengang kommt eine weitere Besonderheit der NDU zum Ausdruck. Sie wendet sich regionalen Fragestellungen zu, rezipiert, diskutiert sie und findet Antworten im internationalen Zusammenhang. Dieser Ansatz der NDU spiegelt sich auch in den Porträts der Personen wider, die in dieser Publikation zu finden sind: regional arbeitende Menschen mit internationaler Erfahrung und Kontakten. Durch sie wird deutlich, dass regionales Arbeiten keinesfalls mit provinziellem Denken verwechselt werden darf!

Ebenso wenig wie Regionalität mit Provinzialität verwechselt werden darf, kann auch „Handwerk" nicht mit standardisiertem und ausschließlich der Tradition verpflichtetem Tun gleichgesetzt werden. In der vorliegenden Publikation wird in besonderer Weise anschaulich dargestellt, dass es gerade die Chance des Handwerks ist, im 21. Jahrhundert die ihm innewohnenden Besonderheiten zu nutzen, die es immer geprägt hat, wie zum Beispiel das autonome und selbstbestimmte Arbeiten mit validen Methoden und Instrumenten. Dies jedoch in Kombination mit forscherischer Neugierde, sich aktuellen, häufig auch sehr komplexen Problemen lösungsorientiert zuzuwenden. Und dies auch im Bewusstsein der sozialen Verantwortung für das Ganze, die damit verbunden ist. In der vorliegenden Publikation wird durch die Autoren und die Porträts von handwerklichen Akteuren zum Ausdruck gebracht, wie dieser Ansatz in Forschung, Studium und Lehre beziehungsweise der handwerklichen Praxis umgesetzt werden kann.

Als Rektor der NDU danke ich den Verantwortlichen für das Zustandekommen dieser zukunftsweisenden Publikation. Sie entspricht auch der Ausrichtung unserer Universität in diesem Bereich unseres Studienangebotes, die wir ebenso als zukunftsweisend erachten: die Erforschung und Entwicklung handwerklicher Methoden und Methodologien sowie die Nutzung der Ergebnisse für die handwerkliche Praxis, aber auch für weitere wissenschaftliche und gestalterische Erkundungen in diesem Bereich.

Manual & Material Culture /
Design, Handwerk & materielle Kultur

The Manual & Material Culture—Design, Handwerk & materielle Kultur degree program was accredited at the New Design University St. Pölten, Austria in September 2013. In October of that same year, only a month later, it was launched with 14 students as passengers and me as its test pilot. By October 2017, 35 students had successfully completed the bachelor's program, and more than 100 students had started the course. Amongst the core subjects mentioned in the German program title—Design, Crafts & Material Culture—it is probably the confident and direct reference to "crafts" that gives our training project its profile and most clearly defines its contrasting approach as compared to other modern design schools and university courses.

But what actually is a thriving, that is economically viable, creative craft in 2017? What is the relationship between design and production in an era when design, production, and distribution tools, and probably also universities, will soon be digitalized? What are the opportunities and potentials that arise from these upheavals for a new generation of manufacturing designers, and for our societies in general?

Manufacturing Design. The "Practice-based Research—Manual & Material Culture" research project used social science methodology to explore how artisanal knowledge (with a focus on designing crafts) from the later part of the 20th century can connect to the changing working and living conditions of the 21st century. Our main interest was to identify the areas of knowledge that can only develop through the threefold role of designer, manufacturer, and marketer.

Our inspirations were personal encounters, in particular with Peter Bruckner, a master locksmith from East Tyrol born in 1935 (p. 19). During our project collaboration in his workshop in Lienz in East Tyrol, and in a number of conversations, he taught me, a person who had only just finished his studies but had already won design awards, more concrete and applicable knowledge about design practice, dealing with customers, and the economization of my creative work, than all of the star design professors, assistant professors, and lecturers I had at art school.

In 2013, this insight led to the idea of systematically documenting and making available such practice-embedded knowledge together with my students, using a research-based learning format. In our context,

Im September 2013 wurde der Studiengang Design, Handwerk & materielle Kultur – Manual & Material Culture an der New Design University St. Pölten akkreditiert. Im Oktober des gleichen Jahres, also ein Monat später, wurde er mit 14 Studierenden als Passagieren und mir als Testpiloten gestartet. Im Oktober 2017 haben 35 Studierende das Bachelorprogramm erfolgreich abgeschlossen und gut 100 Studierende diese Ausbildung begonnen. Von den schon im deutschen Namen „Design, Handwerk & materielle Kultur" genannten Kernthemen des Studiengangs ist wohl der direkte und selbstbewusste Bezug auf „das Handwerk" das, was unserem Ausbildungsprojekt Profil verleiht und uns am schärfsten von anderen zeitgenössischen Designhochschulen und universitären Kursen abgrenzt.

Nur, was ist lebendiges, das heißt ökonomisch tragfähiges, gestaltendes Handwerk im Jahr 2017? In welcher Beziehung stehen Gestaltung und Herstellung in einer Zeit, in der Entwurfs-, Produktions-, Vertriebswerkzeuge und wahrscheinlich auch bald Universitäten digitalisiert sind? Welche Chancen und Möglichkeiten ergeben sich aus diesen Umbrüchen für eine neue Generation produzierender Gestalterinnen und Gestalter und für unsere Gesellschaft im Allgemeinen?

Produzierende Gestaltung. Das Forschungsvorhaben „Practice-based Research – Manual & Material Culture" untersuchte anhand sozialwissenschaftlicher Methoden, wie handwerkliches Wissen (mit Fokus auf gestaltendes Handwerk) aus der zweiten Hälfte des 20. Jahrhunderts Anschluss an die sich verändernde Lebens- und Arbeitswelt des 21. Jahrhunderts finden kann. Dabei interessierte uns besonders, welche Wissensbestände sich nur durch die Personalunion von Entwurf, Herstellung und Vertrieb ausbilden können.

Inspiration dafür waren persönliche Begegnungen und darunter besonders jene mit dem 1935 geborenen Osttiroler Schlossermeister Peter Bruckner (S. 19). Er hat mir, dem schon mit Designpreisen ausgezeichneten gerade nicht-mehr-Studenten, bei der Zusammenarbeit in Projekten in seiner Werkstatt in Lienz/Osttirol und in vielen Gesprächen mehr konkretes und anwendbares Wissen für die Gestaltungspraxis, den Umgang mit Auftraggebern und die Ökonomisierung meiner kreativen Arbeit vermittelt, als meine Design-Starprofessoren, Assistenten und Lektoren an der Kunstuniversität.

Stefan Moritsch
Designer and director of the bachelor's program in Manual & Material Culture at New Design
University St. Pölten, Austria / Designer und Leiter des Studiengangs Design, Handwerk &
materielle Kultur an der New Design University St. Pölten, Österreich

producing designers are understood to be individuals who design, manufacture, and market on a small scale in order to earn their livelihood. This includes in particular craftspeople, designer-makers, and an emerging group of entrepreneurs who come from diverse educational backgrounds and combine design work, technology, and production in order to develop self-determined and economically viable living and working models.

Knowledge in Design. In contrast to design knowledge in design and architecture, the knowledge held by crafters is rarely addressed. The reason for this, besides the division of labor in industrial processes and the separation of design and production it entails, can also be traced to the efforts of designers to establish their discipline as an independent creative discipline in the 20th century. If we consider selected works of often anonymous manufacturing designers, and question their authors about their background, however, we can tap into a knowledge that has been distilled from ongoing practice and that can only emerge when one also manufactures one's design; when design and production are simultaneous processes; when, in addition to the design, production aspects are already considered in the concept, and sometimes new techniques must even be developed for its realization; and when the responsibility for the economic success of projects is assumed by the craftsperson!

Fig. / Abb. 1

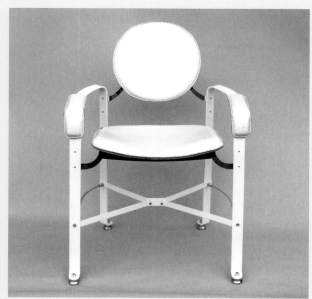

Aus dieser Einsicht entstand 2013 die Idee, im Rahmen forschungsbasierter Lehre systematisch und gemeinsam mit meinen Studierenden dieses in der Praxis gelagerte Wissen zu dokumentieren und zugänglich zu machen. Als produzierende Gestalterinnen und Gestalter werden in diesem Zusammenhang generationenübergreifend Personen verstanden, die in kleinen Strukturen entwerfen, produzieren und vertreiben und davon ihren Lebensunterhalt bestreiten. Darunter fallen insbesondere Handwerkerinnen und Handwerker, Designer-Maker und jene sich aktuell ausbildende Gruppe an Entrepreneure, die mit unterschiedlichsten Bildungshintergründen gestalterische Arbeit, Technologie und Produktion verbinden, um selbstbestimmte und ökonomisch tragfähige Arbeits- und Lebensmodelle zu entwickeln.

Wissen im Entwurf. Im Unterschied zum Entwurfswissen in Design und Architektur wird jenes von Handwerkerinnen und Handwerkern wenig diskutiert. Dies hat neben der durch arbeitsteilige, industrielle Prozesse bedingten Trennung von Entwurf und Produktion auch die Emanzipations- und Profilierungsbestrebungen des Designs als eigenständige Gestaltungsdisziplin im 20. Jahrhundert als Ursache. Betrachtet man ausgewählte Arbeiten oft anonymer produzierender Gestalterinnen und Gestalter und befragt die Autoren zu deren Hintergrund, erschließt sich jedoch ein durch stetige Praxis verdichtetes Wissen, das sich nur ausbilden kann, wenn man den eigenen Entwurf auch fertigt beziehungsweise wenn Entwurf und Herstellung simultan ablaufen; wenn neben der gestalterischen Dimension auch Produktionsaspekte schon bei der Konzeption berücksichtigt und gegebenenfalls neue Techniken für die Umsetzung entwickelt werden müssen; wenn die Verantwortung für den ökonomischen Erfolg der Projekte selbst getragen werden muss!

Zur Veranschaulichung dieses Entwurfswissens kann hier exemplarisch ein Armlehnstuhl von Peter Bruckner aus dem Jahr 1998 (Abb. 1) dienen. Der Stuhl entstand nicht nach einer Entwurfszeichnung, sondern anhand eines 1:1-Arbeitsmodells im Originalmaterial. Die bewusste Rationalisierung des Herstellungsprozesses, das Vermeiden arbeitsintensiver und obsoleter handwerklicher Techniken, der pragmatische Einsatz neuer Technologien sowie Bezüge auf die Designgeschichte prägen dabei Bruckners Arbeit.

Technologie und lebendiges Handwerk. Technologie und lebendiges Handwerk bedingen einander. Handwerker und Designer sind pragmatisch, wenn es um

An armchair by Peter Bruckner from 1998 (fig. 1) may serve as an illustration of such design knowledge. The chair wasn't the result of a design drawing, but of a 1:1 working model in the original material. Bruckner's work is characterized by a conscious rationalization of the manufacturing process, the avoidance of work-intensive and obsolete artisanal techniques, the pragmatic use of new technology, and references to the history of design.

Technology and Thriving Crafts. Technology and thriving crafts rely upon each other. Crafters and designers are pragmatic in matters of integrating technology into their creative work and the related key aspect of livelihood. Digitalization of design, manufacturing, and marketing methods reconnect manufacturing and design. The separation of these areas in the course of industrialization seems to dissolve in the post-industrial era, and manufacturing design on a small scale seems once again possible. Here we can observe that qualities ascribed to crafts, for instance what is called "implicit knowledge", which apparently can only be inscribed into the body by repeated manual work with the materials, declines in favor of a competent use of digital planning tools. The CNC milling machine has long achieved a degree of "industrial" perfection and efficiency—when operating properly—that traditional crafts were never able to attain. Not to mention other numerically controlled methods such as 3-D printing; its application in production is yet in infancy. However, for all our enthusiasm for new technologies and materials, we must not overlook that the indispensable precondition for the development of revolutionary production technology is a deep artisanal understanding of materials and their manipulation, something which involves all human senses.

Transfer of Knowledge. The competencies of producing designers are diverse, for instance in terms of their design methods, problem-solving strategies, technologies, materials, purchasing, and marketing. Here we can observe that in the younger generation, the digitalization of design, production, and marketing, the necessity of a new consumer ethics, and the possibility of global networking are seen as opportunities. In order to exploit them, these individuals need exceptional qualifications in the fields of technology, craftsmanship, economy, and design. This complex knowledge profile cannot be acquired through traditional educational careers. The paradigm that only higher secondary education or academic titles will provide a chance at social advance-

die Integration von Technologie in ihre gestalterische Arbeit und die damit verbundene zentrale Frage der Existenzsicherung geht. Die Digitalisierung von Entwurfs-, Herstellungs-, und Vertriebsmethoden rückt Produktion und Gestaltung wieder näher aneinander. Die Trennung dieser Bereiche im Laufe der Industrialisierung scheint sich im postindustriellen Zeitalter aufzulösen und produzierende Gestaltung in kleinen Strukturen wieder zu ermöglichen. Dabei ist zu beobachten, dass dem Handwerk zugeschriebene Qualitäten, wie das sogenannte implizite Wissen, das sich nur durch stetige manuelle Arbeit am Material dem Körper einzuschreiben scheint, zugunsten der Kompetenz im Umgang mit digitalen Planungswerkzeugen abnimmt. Die CNC-Fräse erreicht schon lange – bei richtiger Ansteuerung – einen Grad an „industrieller" Perfektion und Effizienz, der dem „traditionellen" Handwerk nie möglich war. Ganz abgesehen von anderen numerisch kontrollierten Verfahren wie dem 3D-Druck, dessen Einsatz als Produktionsmittel erst in den Kinderschuhen steckt. Bei aller Begeisterung für neue Technologien und Materialien darf dabei aber nicht übersehen werden, dass die unabdingbare Voraussetzung für die Entwicklung revolutionärer Produktionstechnologien ein tiefes handwerkliches und alle menschlichen Sinne einbeziehendes Verständnis für Werkstoffe und deren Bearbeitung ist. Oder anders gesagt: Wer ein Material und dessen Eigenschaften nicht fühlen kann, kann auch keine Maschine bauen, die es verarbeitet.

Wissenstransfer. Die Kompetenzen produzierender Gestalterinnen und Gestalter sind vielfältig, zum Beispiel bezüglich ihrer Entwurfstechniken, Problemlösungsstrategien, Technologien, Materialien sowie der Akquise und Vermarktung. Dabei ist zu beobachten, dass die jüngere Generation die Digitalisierung von Entwurfs-, Produktions- und Vertriebsmethoden, die Notwendigkeit einer neuen Ethik des Konsums und die Möglichkeit zur globalen Vernetzung als Chance begreift. Um diese zu nutzen, braucht sie außerordentliche Qualifikationen in technologischer, handwerklicher, ökonomischer und gestalterischer Hinsicht. Dieses komplexe Wissensprofil wird nicht in klassischen Bildungslaufbahnen erworben. Das Paradigma, dass nur ein höherer Schulabschluss beziehungsweise akademische Titel gesellschaftliche Aufstiegschancen ermöglichen, führt sich spätestens dann ad absurdum, wenn sich Hochschulabsolventen die Arbeit von Handwerkern und Designern nicht mehr leisten können.

ment is rendered absurd when university graduates can no longer afford the work of craftspeople and designers.

The biographies that today lead to entrepreneurship with a focus on design and manufacturing are extremely complex. More and more often, entrepreneurs drop out of an academic career that can offer them neither economic nor content-related satisfaction, and turn to crafting after years at the university. Conversely, young people with a vocational training in crafts and some work experience seek tertiary education in order to develop further.

Without a hint of sentimentality, we do not believe that crafts and design as we know them from the 20th century will continue to exist in the long run. There is, however, hope that this new generation of manufacturing designers will reach a "critical innovative mass" that will contribute to a sustainable transformation of our society and of our economic system.

Craft-based Design. In the course of the "Practice-based Research—Manual & Material Culture" research project, early on we had the idea to present selected individuals and their design oeuvre in a book. High-quality photographic material of their work, their workshops, and the stakeholders were combined with interviews from the research project condensed into essays to form a contemporary book. The Craft-based Design publication does not claim to provide a comprehensive presentation of the status quo of producing design, but aims instead to acknowledge creative production in the crafts of the late 20th and early 21st centuries as an independent position, and to contrast it with works of design and architecture with which it can easily compare.

Die Biografien, die heute in ein Unternehmertum mit Schwerpunkt Gestaltung und Produktion führen, sind sehr komplex. Immer öfter steigen Entrepreneure aus einer akademischen Laufbahn aus, die ihnen weder ökonomische noch inhaltliche Selbstverwirklichung ermöglicht, und gehen nach Jahren an der Universität ins Handwerk. Umgekehrt streben junge Menschen mit Handwerksausbildung und Berufserfahrung tertiäre Ausbildungen an, um sich weiterzuentwickeln.

Ob es in absehbarer Zeit Handwerk und Design, wie wir es aus dem 20. Jahrhundert kennen, noch geben wird, darf ohne jede Sentimentalität bezweifelt werden. Es besteht aber die Hoffnung, dass die neue Generation produzierender Gestalterinnen und Gestalter eine „kritisch-innovative Masse" erreicht, die zu einer nachhaltigen Veränderung unserer Gesellschaft und unseres ökonomischen Systems beitragen wird.

Craft-based Design. Begleitend zum Forschungsprojekt „Practice-based Research – Manual & Material Culture" entstand sehr bald die Idee, neben dem wissenschaftlichen Forschungsprojekt ausgewählte Persönlichkeiten und ihr gestalterisches Werk in einem Sachbuch zu präsentieren. Hochwertiges Bildmaterial der Arbeiten, der Werkstätten und Akteure wurde in Verbindung mit den zu Texten verdichteten Interviews aus dem Forschungsprojekt zu einer zeitgemäßen Veröffentlichung zusammengestellt. Die Publikation „Craft-based Design" stellt nicht den Anspruch, eine umfassende Darstellung des Status quo in der produzierenden Gestaltung zu geben. Sie hat das Ziel, gestalterische Produktion im Handwerk des ausgehenden 20. und beginnenden 21. Jahrhunderts als eigenständige Position zu würdigen und Werken des Designs und der Architektur als zumindest gleichwertig gegenüberzustellen.

Professional Identities and Intergenerational Change / Berufsidentitäten im Generationenwandel

Changing Crafts. Whenever academics bring up crafts, they tend to become prey to a certain nostalgia. The traditional values and skills of old craftsmanship, from their perspective, seems to be on the decline, a dying métier. This leads to a desire, or even a need, to revive skilled crafts, to "save" them.

A glance at sober statistics, however, shows that the "trades and crafts" sector is still the largest in the Austrian Chamber of Commerce, despite the economic restructuring observed in recent decades. In 2006, nearly a third (31 %) of all private, non-industrial businesses were part of the sector (cf. AWS 2007[1]). Admittedly, this also includes fields that lend themselves less to nostalgic idealization, such as construction and hairdressing salons. On the other hand, many of the positive aspects commonly associated with trades and crafts can today increasingly be found under the label of the "creative industries". The creative industry encompasses the creation, production, dissemination, and media distribution of creative and cultural commodities and services. The creative economy thus includes creative craft sectors, but also designers, architects, and musicians. Questions relating to the transformation of these crafts concern less their supposed demise but rather their definition.

An increasing digitalization and technologization dissolves the limits between design and execution, between creative work and craftsmanship. This transformation involves a new organization of practices as well as of identities. With the socialization of these professions, new professional identities develop and are co-produced. In this chapter, we would like to show how the identities of these craftspeople have changed.

Generations from a Sociological Perspective. Sociologist Karl Mannheim already addressed "The Problem of Generations" in 1928. He postulated that, in reality, any societal change is a generational change. According to him, it is not the zeitgeist per se that changes, but the internal orientation and objectives (generational entelechy) of a birth cohort.

While "generations", in our everyday understanding, are associated with people born within a certain time span, the definition proposed by Mannheim and other generational researchers is more specific. It includes aspects

Handwerk im Wandel. Wenn sich AkademikerInnen mit dem Handwerk beschäftigen, so bemächtigt sich ihrer oftmals eine gewisse Nostalgie. Das alte Handwerk mit seinen traditionellen Werten und Fähigkeiten erscheint aus dieser akademischen Perspektive als im Niedergang begriffen, als aussterbendes Metier. Daraus entwickelt sich der Wunsch, ja, das Bedürfnis, das Handwerk wiederzubeleben, es zu „retten".

Ein Blick auf die nüchterne Statistik zeigt jedoch, dass die Sparte „Handwerk und Gewerbe" trotz des in Österreich in den letzten Jahrzehnten zu beobachtenden wirtschaftlichen Strukturwandels immer noch die größte Sparte in der Wirtschaftskammer darstellt. 2006 gehörte knapp ein Drittel (31 %) aller privaten, nicht-wirtschaftlichen Unternehmen dieser Sparte an (vgl. AWS 2007[1]). Zu dieser Sparte zählen allerdings auch Branchen, die seltener nostalgisch verklärt werden, wie etwa das Baugewerbe und Friseursalons. Viele der positiven Aspekte, die allgemein mit dem Handwerk assoziiert werden, finden sich dagegen heute zunehmend unter der Bezeichnung der „Kreativwirtschaft". Diese umfasst die Schaffung, Produktion, Verteilung und/oder mediale Verbreitung kreativer und kultureller Güter und Dienstleistungen. Kreativwirtschaft schließt somit kreative Handwerkssparten ein, aber auch beispielsweise DesignerInnen, ArchitektInnen oder MusikerInnen. Bei Fragen des Wandels von Handwerk geht es weniger um sein vermeintliches Aussterben, als um seine Definition.

Durch zunehmende Digitalisierung und Technologisierung lösen sich Grenzen zwischen Entwurf und Ausführung, zwischen kreativer und handwerklicher Arbeit auf. Mit diesem Wandel geht sowohl eine neue Gestaltung der Praxis als auch der Identität einher. Mit der beruflichen Sozialisation der Personen entwickeln sich neue Berufsidentitäten, die von ihnen mitproduziert werden. In diesem Kapitel wollen wir aufzeigen, wie sich diese Handwerksidentitäten wandeln.

Generationen aus soziologischer Perspektive. Der Soziologe Karl Mannheim nahm sich bereits 1928 dem „Problem der Generationen" an. Er postuliert, dass jeder gesellschaftliche Wandel tatsächlich ein Generationenwandel ist: Demnach ändert sich nicht der Zeitgeist per se, sondern die innere Orientierung und Zielsetzung („Generationsentelechien") einer Geburtskohorte. Während „Generationen" im Alltagsverständnis mit

---

1 AWS (2007) Gewerbe Handwerk. Daten und Fakten zum österreichischen Gewerbe und Handwerk. Vienna: AWS/WKO.

1 AWS (2007) Gewerbe Handwerk. Daten und Fakten zum österreichischen Gewerbe und Handwerk. Wien: AWS/WKO.

Anna Wanka
Postdoctoral researcher at Goethe University Frankfurt, Germany /
Postdoktorandin an der Goethe-Universität Frankfurt am Main

Julia Pintsuk-Christof
Research associate at New Design University St. Pölten, Austria /
Wissenschaftliche Mitarbeiterin an der New Design University
St. Pölten, Österreich

of time as well as a similar socialization and the simultaneous experience of critical events. Out of this common experiential space, generations form their own orientations and social consciousness (cf. Mannheim 1952[2]). Generational research therefore focuses on different professional socializations and the generational identities arising from them.

Socialization in Past and Present Craftsmanship—The Results of the Research Project "Practice-Based Research — Manual & Material Culture". In the research project "Practice-Based Research—Manual & Material Culture" carried out at the New Design University (NDU) and the University of Vienna, and funded by the State of Lower Austria, the focus was on people whose professional socialization took place during, and who were or still are professionally active, the 20th and 21st centuries[3]. It centered, on the one hand, on the question of how artisanal knowledge from the later half of the 20th century can connect to the changed conditions of life and work of the 21st century. On the other hand, the project also focused on the differences and similarities between the different generations[4] of designer-producers. Below, we provide a comparative presentation of key results[5].

Career Choice. A first generational differentiation can be made according to the question of how a craftsperson came to choose their profession. In the older generation, nearly all respondents became acquainted with their craft through their family environment—the profession had often been, in a sense, "inherited". It was less a question of whether to learn a craft than which one to learn. The decisive factors were economic considerations, the employment situation and the local availability of apprenticeships. For the respondents, the paramount consideration was less to attain self-realization in their chosen profession but more about learning a profession in order to independently earn a living.

Personen, die in einem bestimmten Zeitraum geboren sind, assoziiert werden, ist die Definition bei Mannheim und anderen GenerationenforscherInnen konkreter. So sind sowohl zeit-räumliche Aspekte als auch eine ähnliche Sozialisation und das simultane Erleben kritischer Ereignisse von Bedeutung. Aus diesem gemeinsamen Erfahrungsraum bilden Generationen eigene Orientierungen und ein eigenes soziales Bewusstsein (vgl. Mannheim 1928[2]). Generationenforschung fokussiert folglich die unterschiedliche berufliche Sozialisation und die daraus erwachsenden generationalen Identitäten.

Die Sozialisation ins Handwerk gestern und heute – Ergebnisse des Forschungsprojekts „Practice-Based Research – Manual & Material Culture". Im Rahmen des vom Land Niederösterreich geförderten Forschungsprojekts „Practice-Based Research – Manual & Material Culture" der New Design University (NDU) und der Universität Wien wurde der Fokus auf Personen gerichtet, die im 20. und 21. Jahrhundert beruflich sozialisiert wurden und beruflich aktiv waren oder sind.[3] Dabei stand zum einen im Zentrum, wie handwerkliches Wissen aus der zweiten Hälfte des 20. Jahrhunderts Anschluss an veränderte Lebens- und Arbeitsbedingungen des 21. Jahrhunderts finden kann. Zum anderen war von Interesse, welche Differenzen und Ähnlichkeiten sich zwischen den verschiedenen Generationen[4] produzierender GestalterInnen zeigen. Im Folgenden werden zentrale Ergebnisse vergleichend dargestellt.[5]

Berufsfindung. Eine erste generationale Unterscheidung lässt sich anhand der Frage treffen, wie HandwerkerInnen zu ihrem Beruf gekommen sind. In der älteren Generation kamen beinahe alle befragten Personen durch das familiäre Umfeld mit ihrem Handwerk in Berührung – der Beruf wurde häufig gewissermaßen „vererbt". Es stellte sich weniger die Frage, ob ein Handwerk erlernt werde, sondern vielmehr welches. Dabei waren ökonomische Überlegungen, die Arbeitsmarktsituation und das regionale Angebot an Lehrstellen maßgeblich. Für die Befragten stand

2   Mannheim, Karl (1952) The Problem of Generations. In: Kecskemeti, Paul (ed.) Essays on the Sociology of Knowledge: Collected Works, Volume 5. New York: Routledge, pp. 276-322.

3   In the project, a total of 58 usable, problem-centered narrative biographic interviews were conducted with people between the ages of 27 and 85.

4   For pragmatic reasons, the younger generation was delimited to include craftspeople and creative profession between 25 and 50 years of age, the older generation to people aged 55 and up. This leads to certain overlaps, which have been taken into account.

5   We are planning a separate book on this project, to be published in 2018–2019.

2   Mannheim, Karl (1928) Das Problem der Generationen. In: Kölner Vierteljahreszeitschrift für Soziologie 7, (1928), S. 157-185.

3   Insgesamt wurden 58 verwertbare problem-zentrierte, narrativ-biografische Interviews mit Personen zwischen 27 und 85 Jahren geführt.

4   Aus teils pragmatischen Gründen wurde die jüngere Generation auf HandwerkerInnen bzw. KreativberuflerInnen zwischen 25 und 50 Jahren, die ältere Generation auf ab 55-Jährige eingegrenzt. Dadurch ergeben sich gewisse Überschneidungen, die berücksichtigt wurden.

5   Für 2018/2019 ist eine eigene Buchpublikation zum Projekt geplant.

"I came to shoemaking because I asked a shoe-maker whether he had some home-based work for me, because it wasn't possible to earn a living with the work I was doing before that [...]"
(Cobbler, m, 58)

Our research also highlighted the role of dominant gender stereotypes, which were only rarely questioned. Thus, women tended to opt for the textile sector, men for wood- or metalworking.

In the younger generation, too, there often were familial connections with the chosen craft. However, there was a huge difference in the families' assessment of crafts and trade: Even when the father or mother was also a craftsperson, children often had to assert their choice of a creative profession against parental resistance. The parent generation frequently voiced concerns, for instance, about the ongoing existence of the profession, or its profitability.

"Absolutely mad to start my own business. After all, I had had the perfect life before, in their eyes."
(Picture frame designer, f, 41)

The decision to undertake an apprenticeship was much more often described as an active decision in the younger generation. The inner desire to live one's own creativity and to find fulfillment in it was generally valued higher than economic concerns.

"Because I realized that art had become so important in my life, I said that I will always need to have a creative job. [...] Wow, even if I only have one slice of bread and cheese to eat every day because I don't have any money, it has to be!"
(Bag designer, m, 35)

Educational Biography. Nostalgic ideas of craftsmanship are often accompanied by the idea of straightforward educational and professional biographies. This, however, was not confirmed in our sample: Our respondents interrupted or suspended their apprenticeships, transferred to other crafts, worked intermittently, or restarted training in a different field. In spite of this precariousness, the period of apprenticeship still played a significant role as an institutionalized instance of socialization. It was described as an enormously influential period, in which the respondents were introduced to the joys, but also the woes of their chosen professions. What also

weniger die Selbstverwirklichung im Wunschberuf als das Erlernen eines Berufs für die selbstständige Erwirtschaftung des Lebensunterhalts im Vordergrund.

„Ich bin deswegen zum Schuhmachen gekommen, weil ich gefragt habe, diesen Schuhmacher, ob er eine Heimarbeit für mich hat, weil man durch diese Arbeit, die ich vorher getan habe, das Leben nicht leisten konnte [...]" (Schuhmacher, 58)

Deutlich wurde dabei auch die Rolle vorherrschender Geschlechtsstereotypen, die nur selten hinterfragt wurden. So entschieden sich Frauen tendenziell eher für die Textilbranche, Männer eher für die Holz- oder Metallverarbeitung.

Auch bei der jüngeren Generation gab es häufig familiale Bezugspunkte zum Handwerk. Ein großer Unterschied zeigte sich jedoch in der familialen Bewertung des Handwerks: Selbst wenn Vater oder Mutter auch HandwerkerInnen waren, mussten die Kinder ihren kreativen Berufswunsch häufig gegen deren Widerstände durchsetzen. So äußerte die Elterngeneration nicht selten Bedenken gegenüber dem Bestehenbleiben der Berufsbranche oder deren finanzieller Lukrativität.

„Total wahnsinnig, dass ich mich selbständig mache. Ich hab ja das schönste Leben vorher gehabt in ihren Augen." (Bilderrahmendesignerin, 41)

Die Ausbildungsentscheidung wurde von der jüngeren Generation viel stärker als eine aktive Entscheidung beschrieben. Der innere Wunsch, die eigene Kreativität auszuleben und sich selbst zu verwirklichen, wurde ökonomischen Überlegungen zumeist übergeordnet.

„Weil ich habe gemerkt, dass die Kunst in meinem Leben so was Wichtiges geworden ist, dass ich gesagt habe, ich muss immer kreativ arbeiten [...] wow, selbst wenn ich nur ein Käsebrot am Tag essen kann, weil ich kein Geld habe, aber das muss sein!" (Taschendesigner, 35)

Bildungsbiografie. Mit nostalgischen Vorstellungen über das Handwerk geht häufig eine Vorstellung von geradlinigen Bildungs- und Berufsbiografien einher. Dies bestätigte sich in unserer Stichprobe jedoch nicht: Unsere Befragten unterbrachen Lehren oder brachen diese ab, wechselten in eine andere Handwerksbranche, arbeiteten eine Zeit lang oder begannen eine

became clear was what Richard Sennett[6] described as an incorporation of implicit knowledge, i.e. learning and physical internalization of skills through routine and repetition. The training period was characterized by a clear, hierarchical situation of apprenticeship in which the execution of tasks was superordinate to expressing one's own creativity. There was hardly any space for personal professional development.

> "In reality we were used as unskilled labor, and there was a strict hierarchy: The boss talks, and you don't have any say at all. You weren't allowed to suggest anything or express any wishes, you didn't have any rights at all." (Glazier, m, 70)

The incorporation of skills was often driven by physical punishment:
> "And I was afraid for my life [...] there. I even was beaten to the point of being hospitalized twice in my apprenticeship" (Locksmith, m, 85)

In the younger generation, too, we found non-linear, fragile educational biographies. People followed different educational paths, from apprenticeships to academic studies, to learn their craft or their creative profession. This generation, however, attributes much less importance to the period of training—it only marginally entered into their accounts, and when it did, the context was orientation rather than internalization. Because of the possibility to try different fields, changing educational paths, international experiences, and different (parallel) employments, respondents experienced the period of training more as varied than as repetitive.

> "Later I started art school again [...] Art school is a great way to simply look around during the orientation year, to find out what you really want to do, what direction you want to take." (Printmaker, m, 27)

Professional Biography. The narrow structures of vocational training finally kindled the desire in some respondents of the older generation to become "their own masters" and to start their own business.

They often acquired an aspiration to self-realization at a later date, which many of the younger respondents had already started their education and professional lives with, in their dealings with customers. Their motivation

neue Ausbildung. Trotz dieser Prekarität spielte die Lehrzeit als institutionalisierte Sozialisationsinstanz eine große Rolle. Sie wurde als überaus prägende Zeit beschrieben, in der die Befragten sowohl Freuden als auch Leiden des Berufs erfahren haben. Deutlich wurde hier auch, was schon Richard Sennett[6] als Inkorporation von implizitem Wissen beschrieben hat, nämlich das Erlernen und körperliche Verinnerlichen von Kompetenzen durch Routine und Repetition. Die Ausbildungszeit war durch eine klare, hierarchische Lehrsituation charakterisiert, in der das Ausführen von Arbeitsaufträgen dem Ausleben eigener Kreativität übergeordnet wurde. Der eigenen beruflichen Entfaltung war kaum Raum gegeben.

> „Wir sind dort eigentlich als Hilfsarbeiter missbraucht worden und es hat dort eine Hierarchie geherrscht, der Chef redet und du hast überhaupt nichts zum Sagen. Man konnte dort auch nicht irgendeinen Vorschlag bringen oder irgendeinen Wunsch äußern, man hat da keine Rechte gehabt." (Glaser, 70)

Die Inkorporation von Kompetenzen wurde auch durch körperliche Züchtigung vorangetrieben:
> „Und hab Todesangst [...] dort gehabt. Ich bin halt da zweimal sogar in meiner ganzen Lehrzeit, [...] also krankenhausreif geschlagen worden" (Schlosser, 85)

Auch bei der jüngeren Generation waren brüchige, nichtlineare Bildungsbiografien zu beobachten. Diese absolvierte unterschiedliche Ausbildungen, von Lehre bis zu akademischem Studium, um ihr Handwerk beziehungsweise ihren Kreativberuf zu erlernen. Diese Generation schreibt der Ausbildungszeit jedoch eine deutlich geringere Bedeutung zu – über diese wurde nur marginal berichtet und wenn, dann eher in Zusammenhang mit Orientierung denn Inkorporierung. Durch Möglichkeiten, in verschiedene Bereiche hinein zu schnuppern, wechselnde Ausbildungen, Auslandserfahrungen und unterschiedliche (parallele) Beschäftigungen erlebten die Befragten die Ausbildungszeit als eher abwechslungsreich denn repetitiv.

> „Dann hab ich die Kunstschule wieder angefangen [...] Kunstschule ist eine super Schule, um da mal eben durch dieses Orientierungsjahr einen Zugang

6   See e.g. Sennet, Richard (2008), The Craftsman. New Haven/ London, Yale University Press.

6   Siehe z. B. Sennett, Richard (2008) Handwerk. Berlin: Berlin-Verlag.

for creativity was often the necessity to develop a distinctive style, to create exclusivity in order to succeed in an increasingly competitive market.

> "And then as my business goal I decided that I would do nothing that anybody else did. So, with the same assignment, I would always try and do things differently, to do something new, something that hadn't existed before, even if it was only a small modification, but it should always have a characteristic, a unique distinguishing feature, and that's something that I seem to have managed to continue until today." (Glazier, m, 70)

In the younger generation, we tended to observe the reverse development: They often started with a relatively high aspiration to self-realization, only to learn the necessity of economic calculation through contact with their customers. They then, for instance, accepted commissions they valued less personally because they sold well, or had a sideline as an employee in another business. They also repeatedly reported difficulties in convincing customers of the value of their work. Expertise, in particular in relation to the material or the applied technology, was frequently acquired as implicit incorporated knowledge, but then increasingly explicated in the course of the career into styles or style models. The backdrop of a globalized society in which commodities that were once produced by craftspeople are now industrially produced and/or imported is also an important aspect.

> "Then it was a little difficult because companies came along that were used to ordering things from China; I had to say that I couldn't match those prices. Like, if you order from someone who produces in Austria, you can't expect to get a Chinese price." (Bag designer, m, 35)

Knowledge and Skills of Two Generations of Crafters. What bodies of knowledge and identities did these generational socializations we have outlined above result in? In spite of the diverse socializations of the profession, the focus of both generations is on implicit practical knowledge in the handling of materials.

> "Every day I look at my fabrics; I have a little piece of each fabric I currently use, always with the order number, width, and length and the composition so I can also make the right labels to go with them.

zu finden, was man überhaupt machen will, in welche Richtung es gehen soll." (Druckgrafiker, 27)

Berufsbiografie. Die restriktiven Strukturen des Lehrbetriebs weckten in einigen Befragten der älteren Generation schließlich den Wunsch, ihr „eigener Herr" zu werden und sich selbstständig zu machen.

Den Anspruch zur Selbstverwirklichung, mit dem viele der jüngeren Befragten schon in Ausbildung und Beruf starteten, erwarben sie oftmals erst später im Umgang mit KundInnen. Motivation zur Kreativität war nicht selten die Notwendigkeit, einen eigenen Stil herauszubilden, eine Exklusivität zu schaffen, um auf dem von zunehmender Konkurrenz geprägten Markt bestehen zu können.

> „Und hab mir dann als Unternehmensziel gesetzt, dass ich nichts machen werde, was andere machen. Also bei gleicher Aufgabenstellung werd ich immer versuchen, etwas anders zu machen und etwas Neues zu machen, also etwas, was bisher noch nicht da war, und sei es nur eine kleine Veränderung, aber es sollte immer ein Merkmal haben, ein Alleinstellungsmerkmal haben, und das ist mir offensichtlich bis heute gelungen." (Glaser, 70)

Bei der jüngeren Generation ließ sich eine eher umgekehrte Entwicklung beobachten. So startete diese häufig mit einem relativ starken Selbstverwirklichungsanspruch, musste dann aber im KundInnenkontakt die Notwendigkeit ökonomischer Kalkulation erfahren. Sie nahmen daraufhin etwa von ihnen selbst weniger geschätzte Aufträge an, weil sich diese gut verkaufen ließen oder arbeiteten nebenher in einem Angestelltenverhältnis. Auch wurde immer wieder von Schwierigkeiten berichtet, die KundInnen vom Wert der eigenen Arbeit zu überzeugen. Expertise wurde insbesondere in Bezug auf das Material oder die verwendeten Technologien als implizites, in den Körper eingeschriebenes Wissen erworben, aber im Laufe der Berufstätigkeit zunehmend auch in Stilen beziehungsweise Stilvorbildern expliziert – dies auch vor dem Hintergrund einer globalisierten Gesellschaft, in der früher handwerklich hergestellte Güter heute industriell produziert und/oder importiert werden.

> „Dann war es ein bisschen schwierig, weil da dann so Firmen gekommen sind, die es gewohnt sind, in China zu bestellen, wo ich gesagt habe, den

When I look at them, I get really excited and already know what I will make out of them."
(Fashion designer, f, 34)

Beyond this key competence, for the younger generation proficient self-presentation and networking, for instance by presenting their projects and products on websites, in social media, or at fairs and in the context of competitions, prove to be essential. They also emphasize networking in order to expand the base of potential partners and customers. This already indicates a changed role of digitalization in the crafts of the younger generation: On the one hand, they see the potential of technology to make procedures more efficient and to initiate new creative processes:

"Some methods with films on which you can then produce photos, complex logos, or such things have clearly changed the profession and have almost taken it in a technical direction." (Glass artist, m, 49)

Craftsmanship and modern technology are understood as complementary. This, on the other hand, also highlights a transformation in professional identity—the self-image becomes a blend of technician and designer:

"There are designers who work with 3-D printing, with that plot cutting thingy somehow, and that is craftsmanship, too, when they specialize in one digital method, in a way that in turn results in artisanry." (Bag designer, m, 35)

Conclusion: The Old and New Identities of Crafters.
Crafts are in the midst of a structural, practical, and identity transformation. These can be followed in the interviews we have presented here. For instance, the social organization of socialization in craftsmanship has changed and no longer occurs primarily through the family and in apprenticeship, but often takes place with resistance by the family and through a number of different forms of training and trial and error. The apprenticeship period has lost its key role for the incorporation of artisanal knowledge. However, this does not mean that crafters' skills and identities are acquired in complete freedom. What is often overly emphasized as "maker freedom" (cf. Anderson 2012[7]) in the media—a complete autonomy over methods and products as well as the loss of significance of any qualification other than

7 Anderson, Chris (2012) Makers: The New Industrial Revolution. New York: Crown Business.

Preis kann ich nicht mithalten. Also wenn er bei jemanden, der in Österreich produziert, anfragt, können sie nicht erwarten, dass er einen China-preis bekommt." (Taschendesigner, 35)

Wissen und Kompetenzen zweier Handwerksgenerationen. Zum Aufbau welcher Wissensbestände und Identitäten führen diese generationalen Sozialisationen, die wir in diesem Text skizziert haben? Trotz der unterschiedlichen Sozialisationen in den Beruf steht bei beiden Generationen implizites Praxiswissen um den Umgang mit Material im Zentrum:

„Ich schau mir jeden Tag meine Stoffe an. Ich habe von jedem Stoff, den ich grad benutze, ein kleines Eckerl – da steht auch die Artikelnummer dabei und der Preis und die Breite und die Zusammensetzung, damit ich halt auch die richtigen Etiketten dazu machen kann. Ich schau das an und freu mich halt voll und weiß dann schon, was ich draus machen werde." (Fashiondesignerin, 34)

Über diese Kernkompetenz hinaus zeigen sich bei der jüngeren Generation jedoch kompetente Selbstpräsentation und Vernetzung, etwa durch Präsentation ihrer Projekte und Produkte auf ihren Homepages, in sozialen Medien oder auf Messen und im Rahmen von Wettbewerben, als essenziell. Wert wird außerdem auf Vernetzung gelegt, um den Stamm an potenziell PartnerInnen und KundInnen zu erweitern. Dies deutet bereits auf die veränderte Rolle der Digitalisierung im Handwerk der jungen Generation hin: Technologisierung wird von dieser sowohl als Chance begriffen, Abläufe effizienter zu machen als auch neue kreative Prozesse zu beginnen:

„Gewisse Techniken mit Folien, auf denen man dann eben Fotos herstellen kann, komplizierte Logos oder dergleichen haben sicherlich den Beruf verändert und haben ihn fast zu einer technischen Seite geführt." (Glaskünstler, 49)

Handwerk und moderne Technologien werden als einander ergänzend verstanden. Dadurch zeigt sich andererseits aber auch ein Wandel in den Berufsidentitäten – das Selbstbild verschwimmt zwischen TechnikerInnen und DesignerInnen:

„Es gibt dann schon die Designer, die dann mit 3D-Druck arbeiten, mit dem Plottschnittding irgendwie arbeiten, was ja dann auch wieder Handwerk ist, wenn sie sich so spezialisieren auf diese eine digitale Methode, dass da sozusagen wieder Kunsthandwerk entsteht." (Taschendesigner, 35)

enthusiasm—cannot be deduced from our interviews. Rather, it is likely that other spaces have replaced apprenticeship, in which "communities of practice" (cf. Lave & Wenger 1991[8]) come together and "learn a craft"—in new academic courses and workshops, in shared offices and studios, and on the internet.

These communities of practice consist of people with interdisciplinary backgrounds—graphic designers, fashion designers, technicians, and conventional crafters—and function without the traditional organizational principle of the hierarchy of master and apprentice. The latter is replaced by processes of negotiation in which communication and competent self-presentation are more and more important. In a knowledge society in which knowledge is usually explicable and put into writing, implicit knowledge needs to find new modes of transfer, for instance through YouTube tutorials or fab labs.

We still don't know enough about how and where these learning processes happen outside institutional forms of education and training, and what the role of the "old" generation of crafters plays in them. There is, however, no doubt that they happen and that they open up new creative areas, but also set limits, to the craftsmanship of the future.

8   Lave, Jean; Wenger, Etienne (1991) Situated Learning. Legitimate Peripheral Participation. Cambridge: Cambridge University Press.

Fazit: Alte und neue Handwerksidentitäten. Das Handwerk befindet sich im Struktur-, Praxis- und Identitätswandel. Dies lässt sich anhand der von uns hier exemplarisch dargestellten Interviews nachzeichnen. So hat sich die soziale Organisation der Sozialisation ins Handwerk verändert und erfolgt nicht mehr primär über die Familie in die Lehre, sondern häufig gegen familiale Widerstände und über verschiedenste Ausbildungs- und Ausprobierformen. Die Lehrzeit hat in der Sozialisation ihre zentrale Rolle für die Inkorporation handwerklichen Wissens verloren.

Das bedeutet jedoch nicht, dass handwerkliche Kompetenzen und Identitäten in vollkommener Freiheit erworben werden. Was medial gerne als „maker freedom" (vgl. Anderson 2012[7]) – die vollkommene Autonomie über Arbeitsweise und -produkt sowie der Bedeutungsverlust jeglicher Qualifikationen abseits von Enthusiasmus – überbetont wird, lässt sich aus unseren Interviews nicht ableiten. Viel eher ist anzunehmen, dass an die Stelle der Lehre andere Räume treten, in denen sich „communities of practice" (vgl. Lave & Wenger 1991[8]) zusammenfinden und „Handwerk lernen" – in neuen akademischen Lehrgängen und Workshops, in Gemeinschaftsbüros und -werkstätten sowie im Internet.

Diese „communities of practice" bestehen aus Personen mit interdisziplinären Hintergründen – GrafikerInnen, DesignerInnen, TechnikerInnen und klassischen HandwerkerInnen – und funktionieren ohne das traditionelle Organisationsprinzip der Meister-Lehrling-Hierarchie. An ihre Stelle treten Aushandlungsprozesse, in denen Kommunikation und kompetente Selbstdarstellung wichtiger wird. In einer Wissensgesellschaft, in der Wissen meist explizierbar ist und verschriftlicht wird, muss sich implizites Wissen neue Transferwege suchen – zum Beispiel über Youtube-Tutorials oder FabLabs.

Noch wissen wir viel zu wenig darüber, wie und wo diese Lernprozesse abseits institutioneller Ausbildungsformen stattfinden und welche Rolle die „alte" Handwerksgeneration dabei spielt. Dass sie stattfinden und neue Gestaltungsspielräume, aber auch Grenzen für die Zukunft des Handwerks produzieren, steht jedoch außer Frage.

7   Anderson, Chris (2012) Makers: The New Industrial Revolution. New York: Crown Business.

8   Lave, Jean; Wenger, Etienne (1991) Situated Learning. Legitimate Peripheral Participation. Cambridge: Cambridge University Press.

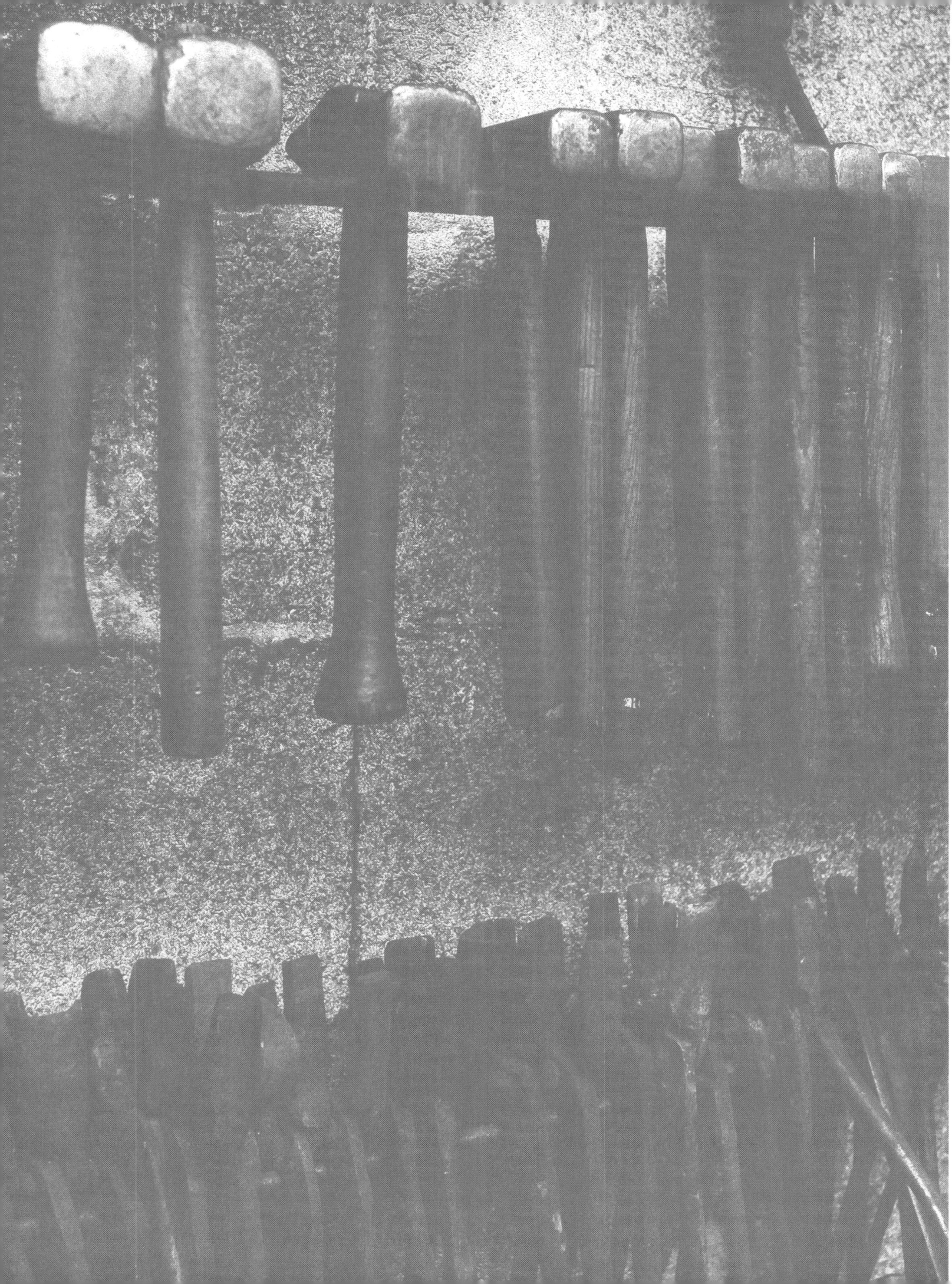

One is for sure. Metalworking is no easy profession. And if you start learning it as a fifteen-year-old five years after WW II in Lienz, East Tyrol, three years later you are journeyman and after three more years you pass the master exam, then you have proved that it wasn't too hard and that you must have discovered and developed a sort of love of this craft. The masterpieces he created as a self-employed from 1956 until today inform eloquently about it.

Eines ist jedenfalls sicher. Die Schlosserei ist kein leichter Beruf. Und wenn man ihn als Fünfzehnjähriger fünf Jahre nach dem Zweiten Weltkrieg im Osttiroler Lienz zu erlernen beginnt, drei Jahre später Geselle ist und noch einmal drei Jahre später die Meisterprüfung ablegt, dann hat man bewiesen, dass es nicht zu schwer war und man zu diesem Handwerk so etwas wie Liebe entdeckt und entwickelt haben muss. Die Meisterstücke, entstanden in der Selbstständigkeit ab dem Jahr 1956 und bis heute, geben beredt Auskunft.

Metal / Metall

Apprenticeship years are no master years. The young apprentice was beaten up day by day. In a way he was the whipping boy. In the three apprenticeship years there wasn't one single day of vacation. The four years of lower grade of gymnasium (secondary school) in Lienz turn out to be a good preparation. The vocational school student is "excellent", and in his grade report he doesn't even have one single "two"[1], nevertheless, due to the unfair beating he's scared to death by the "boss".

1　In Austria, "1" is the highest grade or mark, "2" is the second-best. Tr.n.

Lehrjahre sind keine Herrenjahre. Der Lehrling wurde gleichsam Tag für Tag verprügelt. Er war sozusagen der Prügelknabe. In den drei Lehrjahren gab es keinen Tag Urlaub. Die vier Jahre in der Unterstufe des Lienzer Gymnasiums erweisen sich als gute Vorbereitung. Der Berufsschüler ist „ausgezeichnet" und hat im Zeugnis nicht einen einzigen „Zweier", aber wegen der ungerechten Prügel mehrfach Todesangst vor dem „Chef".

The journeyman. When he is twenty years old and journeyman, he is beaten for the last time, because after that he leaves the company, "to never come back again". In the newspaper he reads that Jenbacher Werke, naturally located in Jenbach, is hiring metalworkers. He hits the road and due to the help from a union, that is by a confirmed communist of the holy land Tyrol, all at once he is paid twice as much, that's eight schillings and fifty cents per hour. However, paradise is yet to come.

Der Geselle. Als er zwanzig Jahre alt und Geselle ist, wird er ein letztes Mal verprügelt, weil er danach den Betrieb verlässt, „um nie mehr wieder zu kommen". In der Zeitung liest er, die Jenbacher Werke, naturgemäß in Jenbach, würden Schlosser suchen. Er macht sich auf den Weg und verdient wegen der gewerkschaftlichen Hilfe eines eingefleischten Kommunisten des Heiligen Lands Tirol mit einem Schlag das Doppelte, nämlich acht Schilling fünfzig in der Stunde. Doch das Paradies ist erst im Anzug.

> "A hexagon screw is one
> of the most beautiful
> connecting materials."
> Peter Bruckner

Paradise Switzerland. He follows one of the best art blacksmiths of his time—as a master, already—to Zurich, in order to learn from him. Switzerland seems like paradise to him, where for the first time an actual millionaire becomes available to him. Before he starts working, the money man shows him his entire villa. "Time doesn't matter, it's got to be precise!" In paradise he becomes "Gruezi, Mister Bruckner!" In first-name-only Tyrol an unknown form of address.

Making twice the money. After coming back home, because of the high Swiss payment, twice the Austrian one so to speak, he "no longer wanted to go working as a factory or blue-collar worker" and started "his own enterprise in the garden." In the first three years he "worked outdoors".

The ruler in the kingdom of metal. To him working with wood always wasn't quite enough and it wouldn't have really satisfied him. Handicraft and wood carving didn't

Das Paradies Schweiz. Einem der besten zeitgenössischen Kunstschmiede reist er – bereits als Meister – nach Zürich nach, um von ihm zu lernen. Die Schweiz erscheint ihm als Paradies, in dem für ihn zum ersten Mal ein Millionär greifbar wird. Bevor er mit der Arbeit beginnt, zeigt ihm der Geldmensch seine ganze Villa. „Zit spielt keine Rolle, präzise muss es sein!" Im Paradies wird er zum „Grüezi, Herr Bruckner!" Im Du-Land Tirol eine unbekannte Ansprache.

Der doppelte Verdienst. Nach Hause zurückgekommen, wollte er wegen des hohen Schweizer Verdiensts, sozusagen Österreich mal zwei, „nicht mehr als Arbeiter gehen" und wurde „im Garten selbstständig". Die ersten drei Jahre hat er „im Freien gearbeitet".

Der Herrscher im Königreich Metall. Das Arbeiten mit Holz war ihm immer zu wenig und hätte ihn nicht wirklich befriedigt. Das Basteln und das Schnitzen hätten ihn nicht ausgefüllt. „Ich wollte immer das Metall be-

Dining room chair / Esszimmerstuhl (1998)
On behalf of / Im Auftrag von: Maria Großgasteiger
White powder-coated mild steel with gilded brass elements and
white leather upholstery. / Baustahl weiß pulverbeschichtet mit
vergoldeten Messingelementen und weißer Lederpolsterung.

Metal / Metall

give him fulfilment. "I always wanted to dominate metal."
The different colors of metal. And its use. Preferably
inexpensive steel. Copper for beating-out works, for
example sculptures. The high-polished brass, which you
can chrome or paint gold. And "sheet metal you cannot
beat it out, you can just fold it, like paper."

Artist's pride. The king of metal from Lienz has produced
bedsteads, windows, company logos, store portals,
front doors, the Holy Family in the church, school tables,
tower clocks, spiral staircases and much more. If some-
body wanted to order something he or she had seen at
the neighbor's home he didn't accept the order. "I don't
make the same any longer. I don't copy myself." The
ordering customers were so convinced of his art and
skills that they renounced designs.

herrschen." Die verschiedenen Farben des Metalls. Und
sein Gebrauch. Vorrangig der preiswerte Stahl. Das
Kupfer für Treibarbeiten, beispielsweise Skulpturen. Das
hochglanzpolierte Messing, das man verchromen oder
vergolden kann. Und „Blech darfst Du nicht treiben, nur
falten, wie Papier."

Künstlerstolz. Der Metallkönig von Lienz hat Bettgestelle,
Fenster, Firmenzeichen, (Geschäfts-)Portale, Haustüren,
die Heilige Familie in der Kirche, Schultische, Turmuhren,
Wendeltreppen und vieles andere hergestellt. Wollte
jemand etwas bestellen, das er beim Nachbarn gesehen
hat, hat er den Auftrag nicht angenommen. „Das Gleiche
mache ich nicht mehr. Ich kopiere mich nicht selber." Die
Auftraggeber waren von seinen Künsten derart über-
zeugt, dass sie auf Entwürfe verzichtet haben.

Rohracher Art Nouveau villa / Jugendstilvilla Rohracher (1980)

Peter Bruckner

Rohracher Art Nouveau villa / Jugendstilvilla Rohracher (1980)
On behalf of / Im Auftrag von: Dipl.-Ing. Michael Rohracher
Garden gate with canopy above the entrance area and the terrace. / Garten-
eingangstor mit Überdachung des Eingangsbereichs und der Terrasse.
Realized in untreated mild steel. Surface with natural patina (rust). /
Ausführung: Baustahl unbehandelt. Oberfläche: natürliche Patina (Rost).

The philosophy of iron. If he received an order to make a workpiece for an Art Nouveau villa he knew that he was not allowed to "do any harm" to the house. "You have to work everything Art Nouveau-wise." Nothing may be "shot down in a modern way".

The geography of art. The art of the iron philosopher has gone far and way beyond the city limits of Lienz. You come across it in Berlin, Gstaad, Kitzbühel, Mönchengladbach, Salzburg, Zurich and other places of this world. "The profession must go on" in the first place, even though "the pants are constantly torn and the hands are black all the time".

Die Philosophie des Eisens. Hatte er den Auftrag, für eine Jugendstilvilla ein Werkstück herzustellen, wusste er, er dürfe dem Haus „nicht wehtun". „Du musst alles auf Jugendstil arbeiten." Es darf nichts „modern nieder- geknallt" werden.

Die Geografie der Kunst. Die Kunst des Eisenphiloso- phen ist weit über Lienz hinausgekommen. Man stößt auf sie in Berlin, Gstaad, Kitzbühel, Mönchengladbach, Salzburg, Zürich und anderen Orten dieser Welt. Über- haupt soll „der Beruf weitergehen", obwohl „die Hosen pausenlos zerrissen und die Hände schwarz sind".

Kraler residence / Wohnhaus Kraler (1996)

Kraler residence / Wohnhaus Kraler (1996)
On behalf of / Im Auftrag von: Franz Kraler
Garden gate, garden fence and canopy above the entrance area. Realized in untreated mild steel. Surface with natural patina (rust). / Garteneingangstor, Gartenzaun und Überdachung des Eingangsbereichs. Ausführung: Baustahl unbehandelt., Oberfläche: natürliche Patina (Rost).

Metal / Metall

„Eine Sechskantschraube gehört zu den schönsten Verbindungsmaterialien."
Peter Bruckner

29

Großgasteiger apartment /
Wohnung Großgasteiger
(1986)

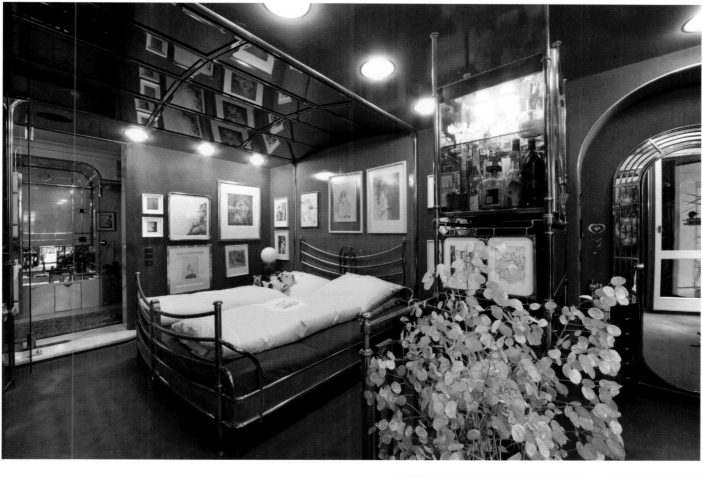

Großgasteiger apartment / Wohnung Großgasteiger (1986)
On behalf of / Im Auftrag von: Maria Großgasteiger
Complete fitting out of the flat. Highlights include the mirrored cabinet with five semicircular drawers on each side, the bookshelf, the house bar, the bed, the bathroom; all in polished brass. / Kompletter Wohnungsausbau. Zu sehen unter anderem der Spiegelschrank mit jeweils fünf seitlichen halbrunden Schubfächern, das Bücherregal, die Hausbar, das Bett, das Badezimmer; alles aus Messing poliert.

31

City Cafe,
Lienz (1986)

Peter Bruckner

City Café (1990)
On behalf of / Im Auftrag von: Gerhard Glanzl
Café furnishings with ceiling lining, visible ventilation system, light fixtures, main entrance and display window. Polished brass, certain elements varnished. / Kaffeehauseinrichtung mit Deckenverkleidung, sichtbarer Belüftung, Beleuchtungskörpern, Eingangsportal und Schaufenster, Messing poliert, Teilelemente lackiert.

Peter Bruckner

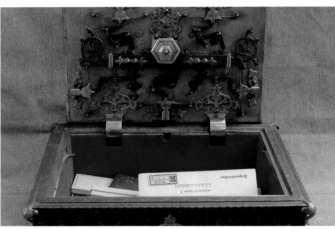

Peter Bruckner's work to qualify as a master locksmith / Meisterstück Peter Bruckner (1956)
On behalf of / Im Auftrag von: Self-commissioned / Eigenauftrag
Steel box engraved with adjustable brass lion's head and secret keyhole, lock with six bolts on the inside and handworked key. / Stahlkassette ziseliert mit verstellbarem Löwenkopf aus Messing und geheimem Schlüsselloch, sechsriegeliger Versperrung im Innenteil und handgearbeitetem Schlüssel.

Peter Bruckner   1935 Born / Geb. in Steinach am Brenner • 1945–1949: Gymnasium Lienz • 1950–1953: Apprenticeship as a locksmith at locksmith company Pedit, Lienz / Schlosserlehre Schlossereibetrieb Pedit, Lienz • 1953: Apprenticeship certification exam / Gesellen-prüfung • 1953–1956: Journeyman years at locksmith company Pedit, Lienz / Gesellenjahre Schlossereibetrieb Pedit, Lienz • 1956: Master craftsman exam / Meisterprüfung • 1956–1958: Machine repairman at Jenbacher Werke / Maschinenreparaturschlosser Jenbacher Werke • 1958–1960: Locksmith at different locksmith companies in Austria and Switzerland / Schlosser in verschiedenen Schlossereibetrieben in Österreich und in der Schweiz • 1961: Returned to Lienz/East Tyrol and opened his own locksmith company; since then continuous freelance work / Rückkehr nach Lienz/Osttirol und Eröffnung eines eigenen Schlossereibetriebes; seither ohne Unterbrechung selbstständig

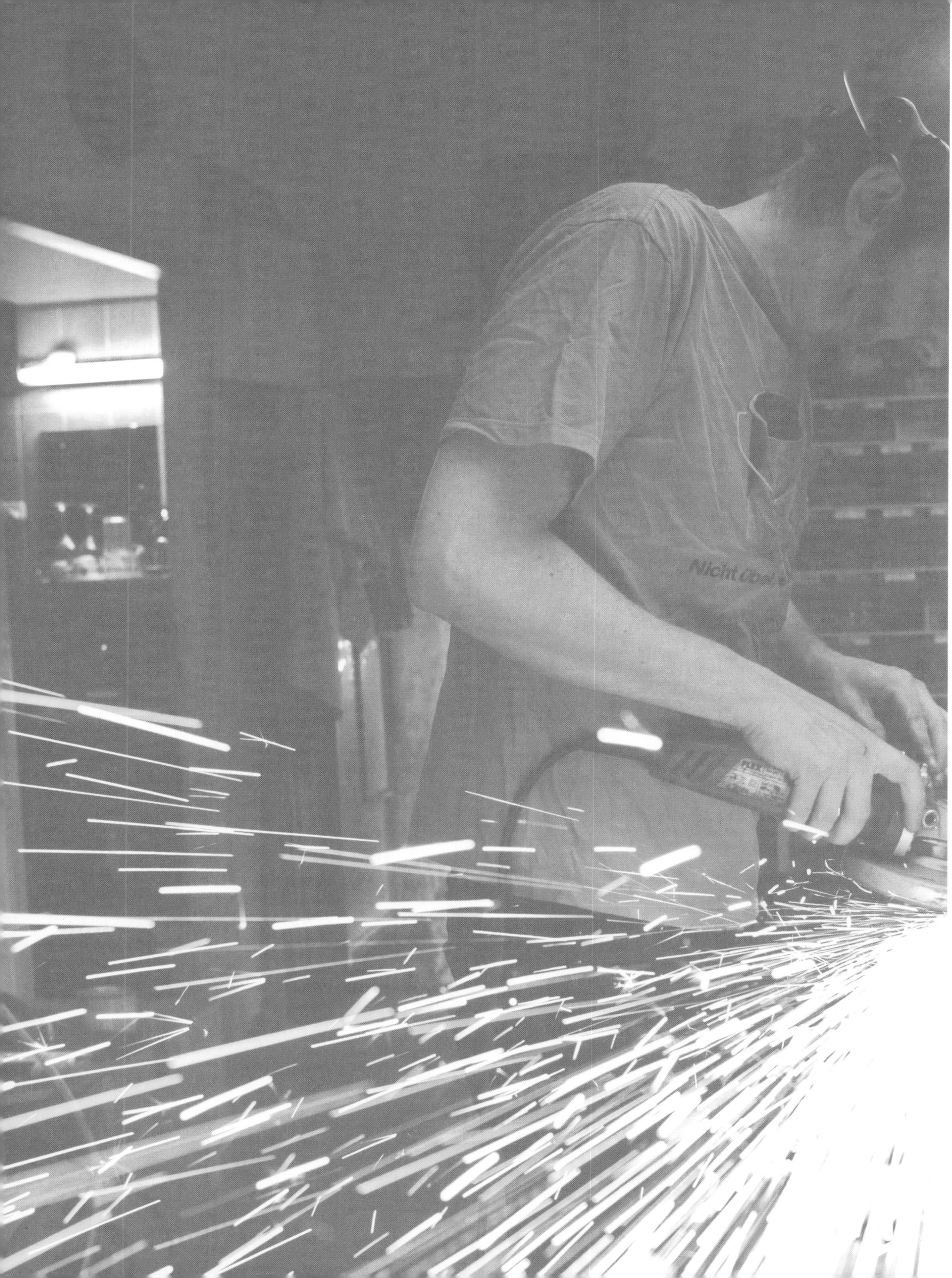
Nicht übel

At the beginning, as an apprentice he learned to make tools at a world-known company. Then in Hohenems he graduated from gymnasium (senior high school) with the *Matura*. Eventually, he studied design, craft and material culture in St. Pölten. As a matter of fact everything, drilling, filing, sawing, how tools work, began due to the grandfather. He was the initial spark, so to speak. Thomas Bernhard, a farmer in his civil profession, has already apodictically determined: "The grandfathers are the teachers, the actual philosophers of every individual."

Am Anfang als Lehrling Werkzeuge machen gelernt bei einem weltbekannten Unternehmen. Dann in Hohenems die Matura absolviert. Schließlich Design, Handwerk und materielle Kultur in St. Pölten studiert. Und eigentlich hat alles, bohren, feilen, sägen, wie Werkzeuge funktionieren, wegen des Großvaters begonnen. Er war gleichsam der Initialzünder. Schon Thomas Bernhard, im Zivilberuf Bauer, hat apodiktisch festgestellt: „Die Großväter sind die Lehrer, die eigentlichen Philosophen jedes Menschen."

Metal / Metall

Thomas Rösler

The grandfathers are the teachers. From his second year of life he was taught by his grandfather in drilling, filing and sawing. He showed to him how tools work. After many not too good grades, continuing gymnasium made "no sense". A position for a tool maker apprentice was specifically looked for and was soon found. He "always liked" working with metal. The material "is not as sensitive as wood, it's more raw and more mangy". Eventually, he stayed for eleven years with the company, in which he has learned for his life."

Die Großväter sind die Lehrer. Ab dem zweiten Lebensjahr wurde er von seinem Großvater im Bohren, Feilen und Sägen unterrichtet. Er hat ihm gezeigt, wie Werkzeuge funktionieren. Nach mehreren nicht sehr guten Noten hatte der weitere Besuch des Gymnasiums „keinen Sinn". Eine Lehrstelle für Werkzeugmacher wurde gezielt gesucht und bald gefunden. Das Arbeiten mit Metall hat ihm „immer schon getaugt". Der Werkstoff „ist nicht so empfindlich wie Holz, er ist gröber und räudiger". Letztlich ist er in der Firma, in der er auch für das Leben gelernt hat, elf Jahre geblieben.

„With steel I enjoy working,
because it's so raw."
Thomas Rösler

Precise top apprenticeship. In retrospect he calls it a top apprenticeship. You learn that "you have to be answerable" for your mistakes and that it's about precision. "Tool maker is an extremely precise profession." Often it's about thousandths of a millimeter. A hair has four hundredths of a millimeter. This is all about feeling", despite the fact that for the craft you need and use the body, that is the entire body.

Präzise Spitzenlehre. Er spricht im Nachhinein von einer Spitzenlehre. Man lernt, dass man für seine Fehler „gerade stehen muss" und es um Präzision geht. „Werkzeugmacher ist ein unheimlich genauer Beruf. Es geht oft um tausendstel Millimeter. Ein Haar hat vierhundertstel Millimeter. Das ist alles eine Gefühlsgeschichte", obwohl man für das Handwerk den Körper, und zwar den ganzen, braucht und einsetzt.

„Mit Stahl arbeite ich gern,
weil er so grob ist."
Thomas Rösler

Lamp / Lampe (2014)
On behalf of / Im Auftrag von: Lights of Vienna
Homage to a lampshade. The lightbulb is replaced by a LED strip of
lights in the brass mounting base. BA project in Manual & Material
Culture. / Hommage an den Lampenschirm. Die Glühbirne wird ersetzt
durch ein LED-Lichtband in der Messingaufhängung. Diplomarbeit
BA in Manual & Material Culture.

Chinese hand-craft. You learn that with trades, that is craft sections, everything is connected, the plumbing, the masonry, the carpenter jobs, and amidst those activities he reads about the study of design, which in the meantime he has graduated in. "I quit my job right away." Four months and an admission test later he was studying and next to that he was in China, where he actually understood what hand-craft is, because only a few machines were available. It was a hand-in-hand way of working, without a language of words, because he didn't speak Chinese and the Chinese didn't speak English. "This way, a tremendous relationship comes about".

After the craft master exam, the master. When he quits from the company he's been working for, the staff manager can't keep him even with "more money". While studying he was enthusiastic about his practical skills receiving a theoretical background. "You get an academic degree on top of the practical knowledge."

Das chinesische Hand-Werk. Man lernt, dass bei den Gewerken alles zusammenhängt, das Klempnern, Mauern, die Zimmermannsarbeiten, und mitten in diesen Tätigkeiten liest er über das Design Studium, das er inzwischen absolviert hat. „Meinen Job habe ich gleich gekündigt." Vier Monate und eine Aufnahmsprüfung später hat er studiert und daneben war er in China, wo er tatsächlich begriffen hat, was Hand-Werk ist, weil nur wenige Maschinen zur Verfügung standen. Es war ein Hand-in-Hand-Arbeiten ohne Wörter-Sprache, weil er nicht Chinesisch und die Chinesen nicht Englisch konnten. „So entsteht eine unheimlich gute Beziehung."

Nach dem Meister der Master. Als er in seiner Firma kündigt, kann ihn die Personalchefin auch mit „mehr Geld" nicht halten. Beim Studium hat ihn begeistert, dass seine praktischen Fähigkeiten einen theoretischen Hintergrund bekommen haben. „Man kriegt zum praktischen Wissen einen akademischen Grad."

Schella Kann Atelier /
Werkstatt Schella Kann
(2014)

Schella Kann Atelier / Werkstatt Schella Kann (2014)
On behalf of / Im Auftrag von: Schella Kann
Atelier and store of the fashion label Schella Kann. Planned and realized
by Thomas Rösler and Dieter Winder. Designed by Conrad Simeon Kroencke. /
Atelier und Geschäft des Modelabels Schella Kann. Planung und Umsetzung
von Thomas Rösler und Dieter Winder. Entwurf: Conrad Simeon Kroencke.

All materials. Earlier he mainly worked with steel, today with all materials. Also with wood, ceramic or plastic. And even with gold, when he made the wedding rings for bridal pairs who were his friends. Steel construction is dirty and soft at the same time. It forgives a lot. Wood does smell good, however, you have to treat it very carefully.

A little bit of an idea. With the materials he is able to manufacture everything that is ordered. Picture frames, kitchens, fair stands, furniture, rings, tables, sinks and, and, and. The nice thing about it is working with people who know what they want "and have a bit of an idea". Who help you with their own ideas with the "designer stuff". It's about people who want something special and receive something special.

Alle Werkstoffe. Hauptsächlich hat er früher mit Stahl gearbeitet, heute mit allen Werkstoffen. Auch mit Holz, Keramik oder Plastik. Und sogar Gold, wenn er für befreundete Brautpaare die Eheringe gefertigt hat. Der Stahlbau ist dreckig und geschmeidig zugleich. Er verzeiht vieles. Holz riecht zwar gut, doch muss man mit ihm sehr vorsichtig umgehen.

Ein bisschen Ahnung. Mit den Werkstoffen kann er alles, was bestellt wird, herstellen. Bilderrahmen, Küchen, Messestände, Möbel, Ringe, Tische, Waschbecken und, und, und. Schön ist dabei die Zusammenarbeit mit Menschen, die wissen, was sie wollen und „ein bisschen eine Ahnung" haben. Die einen mit ihren eigenen Ideen beim „Designerding" unterstützen. Es geht um Leute, die etwas Besonderes wollen und etwas Besonderes bekommen.

Thomas Rösler

KARAK tiles (2015)
On behalf of / Im Auftrag von: KARAK tiles
KARAK, a young tile factory in Vorarlberg, makes clay products that unite tradition and the modern. / KARAK, eine junge Fliesenmanufaktur aus Vorarlberg, fertigt Tonprodukte, die Tradition und Moderne vereinen.

Side tables / Beistelltische (2016)
On behalf of / Im Auftrag von: KARAK tiles

Difficulties to control raku firing regularly produces scrap tiles. Integrated into end tables, these individual pieces find a new use. / Durch den schwer kontrollierbaren Rakubrand entstehen regelmäßig Ausschussfliesen. Integriert in Beistelltische finden diese Einzelstücke eine neue Verwendung.

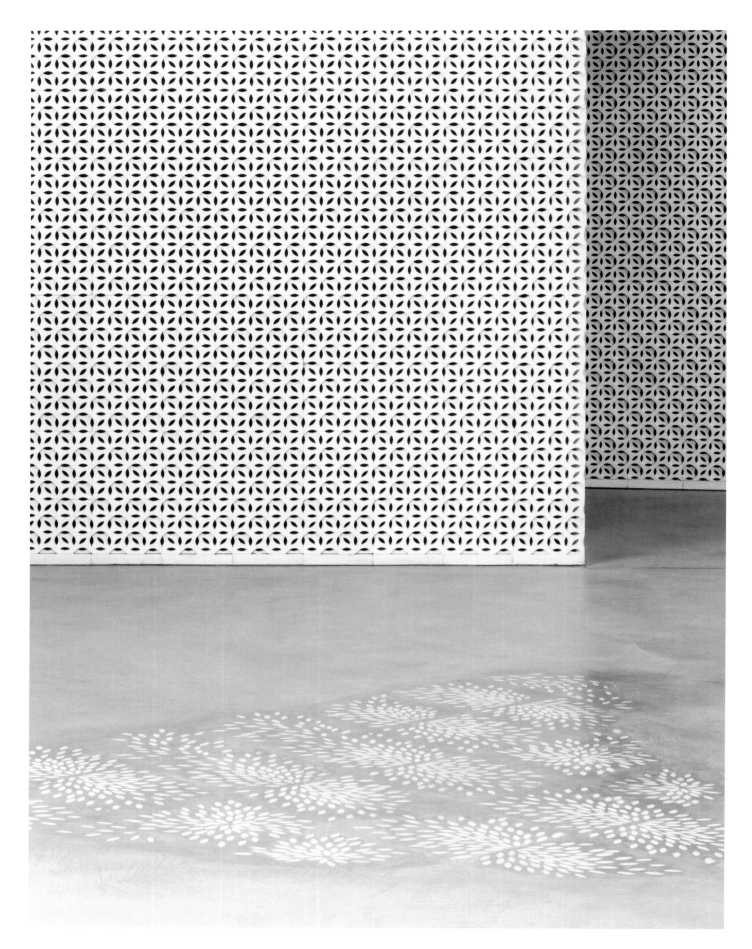

Thomas Rösler

Exemplary works. His particular, that is exemplary works are grid tiles for a concert hall or a huge portal for a fashion label. In these orders, especially the necessity of dovetailing different trades and craft areas fascinated him. In all that he realized that the time factor is always more costly than the material. Moreover, you learn what is exceptionally costly, all the time.

Exemplarische Arbeiten. Seine besonderen beziehungsweise exemplarischen Arbeiten sind Gitterfliesen für eine Konzerthalle oder ein Riesenportal für ein Modelabel. Bei diesen Aufträgen hat ihn besonders die Notwendigkeit der Verzahnung verschiedener Gewerke fasziniert. Dabei hat er erkannt, dass der Faktor Zeit immer kostspieliger ist als das Material. Außerdem lernt man, was ausnehmend kostbar ist, die ganze Zeit.

TaOk 3-D tile / Gitterfliese TaOk (2007)

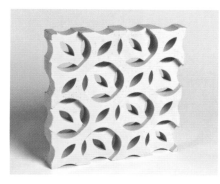

TaOk 3-D tile / Gitterfliese TaOk (2007)
On behalf of / Im Auftrag von: Gönhard School in Aarau / Schule Aarau Gönhard Self-designed and produced sound-absorbing 3-D tiles in cooperation with Marta and Sebastian Rauch and the company Lehm Ton Erde. / In Kooperation mit Marta und Sebastian Rauch sowie der Firma Lehm Ton Erde. Selbst entworfene und produzierte, schallabsorbierende Gitterfliesen.

Metal / Metall

Thomas Rösler

KuQua Hex / X (2007)

On behalf of / Im Auftrag von: Self-commissioned / Eigenauftrag

In 2007 Marta Rauch had the idea to produce raku ceramic tiles in Vorarlberg. This idea was picked up on and expanded by Sebastian Rauch and Thomas Rösler. / Die Idee, Raku-Keramikfliesen in Vorarlberg zu produzieren, wurde 2007 von Marta Rauch geboren, durch Sebastian Rauch und Thomas Rösler aufgegriffen und ausgebaut.

Thomas Rösler   1985 Born / Geb. in Feldkirch • 1996–2001: Bundesgymnasium Bludenz • 2001–2004: Toolmaker apprenticeship at HILTI AG, Thüringen / Werkzeugmacherlehre HILTI AG, Thüringen • 2005–2013: HILTI AG, Thüringen • 2007–2015: Technicalsupport, KARAK, Schlins / Technischer Support, KARAK, Schlins • 2011–2013: University entrance exam (business studies), WIFI Hohenems / Berufsreifeprüfung (BWL), WIFI Hohenems • 2013–2016: Studied Manual & Material Culture at New Design University St. Pölten / Studium Manual & Material Culture, New Design University St. Pölten • 2015: Started freelance work / Beginn der Selbstständigkeit

100
120

Wood isn't just a monosyllabic word. This he realized soon, and therefore, after the mandatory schools, the apprenticeship and community service[1] in a rehabilitation center, first he was journeyman, later production manager, and a selfemployed joiner. He attended a master class in St. Pölten in order to get on the academic path. The interior designer was kind of obvious. Today the original profession is planed down and fine-polished, so that he is able to practice it as an enterprise that is in his own one.

Holz ist nicht nur ein einsilbiges Wort. Was er bald erkannt hat, weshalb er nach Pflichtschule und Lehre samt Zivildienst in einem Rehabilitationszentrum zunächst Geselle, später Fertigungsleiter und selbstständiger Tischler war. Einen Meisterkurs belegte er, um dann in St. Pölten auf den akademischen Holzweg zu gelangen. Der Innenarchitekt war naheliegend. Heute ist der ursprüngliche Beruf gehobelt und feingeschliffen, sodass er ihn sozusagen firmenmäßig, soll heißen im eigenen Betrieb, ausüben kann.

1   The alternative to the [mandatory] military service. (Tr. n.)

Wood / Holz

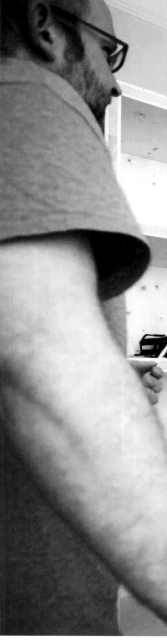

"The raw material wood
gives a feeling of
security and warmth."
Martin Aigner

The apprenticeship was the time of observing. The career in wood really started at the age of fifteen. He doesn't know the reason for his vocation. Joiner was a result. "It was the right thing, the one that fit, that suited me best". For him the apprenticeship was in a way watching, observing the master and the journeyman, by which above all he learned how adults react to challenges. Moreover, it was a sweeping as well as a cleaning. And vocational school was fun. Already then he dreamed about his own business and of being self-employed.

Die Lehre war die Zeit des Beobachtens. Richtig angefangen habe die Karriere in Holz mit fünfzehn. Den Grund seiner Berufung kenne er nicht. Der Tischler habe sich ergeben. „Es war das Richtige, das Passende." Die Lehre war für ihn gewissermaßen ein Zuschauen, ein Beobachten des Meisters und des Gesellen, wodurch er vor allem gelernt habe, wie Erwachsene auf Herausforderungen reagieren. Außerdem war es ein Kehren sowie Putzen. Und die Berufsschule habe Spaß gemacht. Schon damals habe er von der eigenen Firma und Selbstständigkeit geträumt.

The beauty of wood. "I want to solve my daily life efficiently. What results from that is the wish of wanting design-wise and art-wise." That means the link between carpentry and architecture with the raw material wood, which "gives warmth, a sense of security and is perceived as beautiful". With each piece which is cut a decision is taken. Wood is the material "one feels at home most" with. As an apprentice, however, he worked a lot with chipboards which were veneered.

Die Schönheit des Holzes. „Ich will meinen Alltag effektiv lösen. Daraus ergibt sich der Wunsch nach gestalterischem und künstlerischem Wollen." Das heißt, die Verbindung zwischen Tischlerei und Architektur mit dem Rohstoff Holz, der „Wärme vermittelt, Geborgenheit gibt und als schön empfunden wird". Mit jedem Stück, das abgeschnitten wird, treffe man eine Entscheidung. Holz sei das Material, mit dem man sich „am ehesten zuhause fühlt". In der Lehrzeit habe er hingegen viel mit Spanplatten gearbeitet, die furniert worden seien.

KÜBAL (Kitchen, Bath, Luxury) / KÜBAL (Küche, Bad, Luxus) (2013)
On behalf of / Im Auftrag von: Private / Privat
Division of two rooms into different areas of activity with a minimal amount of materials and effort. / Aufteilung zweier Räume in unterschiedliche Funktionsbereiche mit minimalem Material und Arbeitsaufwand.

"Hey, could you make the cupboard cheaper?" The study was a "stage of sorting myself out". Today he mainly makes furniture of synthetic materials. Countless orders come under the motto "Is it possible to get it a little bit cheaper?", which "says much about society." Orders and requests from customers who come to the workshop with photos of products of a world-known Swedish furniture giant in their hand and ask whether he could make the item a bit cheaper are not accepted or rejected. He practices a "small group corporation production and not a large group corporation production."

„Hey, können'S das Kastl billiger machen?" Das Studium sei eine „Findungsphase" gewesen. Heute stelle er vor allem Kunststoffmöbel her. Unzählige Aufträge fallen unter das Motto „Geht's ein bissl billiger?", was „viel über die Gesellschaft aussagt". Aufträge beziehungsweise Anfragen von Kunden, die mit Produktfotos eines weltbekannten schwedischen Möbelriesen in der Hand in die Tischlerei kommen und fragen, ob man das Kastl" billiger herstellen könne, werden nicht angenommen oder abgelehnt. Er betreibe eine „Kleinkonzernproduktion und keine Großkonzernproduktion".

Room in a Room / Raum im Raum (2016)
On behalf of / Im Auftrag von: Das Rund
Room divider, made of wood scraps from his own workshop and additional purchases from the "willhaben" advertising portal. Spontaneously designed and realized on site. / Raumteiler, hergestellt aus Holzresten der eigenen Werkstatt und Zukäufen vom Anzeigenportal „willhaben". Spontan vor Ort entworfen und umgesetzt.

Balance of design and handcrafting. You have to think about how to deal with the wishes and the budget of the customer placing the order in the first place, which is difficult, "because here almost always I am in a dilemma". His biggest customers are a motion picture production company and two architecture[2] offices. Those "as such are counterpoles." He tries to find "the balance between design and craftsmanship" as well as the ideas of the customers. Projects in which many of his ideas can be translated into action are particularly important to him.

Balance von Design und Handwerk. Überhaupt müsse man sich Gedanken darüber machen, wie man mit den Wünschen und dem Budget des Auftraggebers umgehe, was schwierig sei, „weil ich mich da fast immer in einer Zwickmühle befinde". Seine größten Kunden seien eine Filmproduktionsfirma und zwei Architekturbüros. Das seien „an und für sich Gegenpole". Er versuche, „die Balance zwischen Design und Handwerk" sowie den Vorstellungen der Auftraggeber zu finden. Projekte, in denen viele seiner Ideen umgesetzt werden können, seien ihm besonders wichtig.

2   And/or interior design. (Tr. n.)

The shine is expensive. In his opinion the support of handcrafting by computer technology is right. The resulting product is more precise through it. Nevertheless, one must differentiate between handcrafting and industry. In handcrafting robots are not active. In small enterprises "the cutting work is actually done by hand." "I think small industry is very effective". And you can sell anything "that shines" for a high price.

Der Glanz ist teuer. Die Unterstützung des Handwerks durch die Computertechnologie halte er für richtig. Das Ergebnis des Produkts sei dadurch genauer. Unterscheiden müsse man jedoch zwischen dem Handwerk und der Industrie. Im Handwerk würden keine Roboter tätig sein. In den Kleinbetrieben werde „wirklich mit der Hand zugeschnitten". „Die kleine Industrie finde ich sehr effektiv." Und teuer verkaufen könne man alles, „was glänzt".

Patchwork Kitchen 1 (2013)
On behalf of / Im Auftrag von: Private / Privat
Patchwork design integrates the resources of the individual who commissioned the piece such as time, old furniture or money into the design and realization. Creative spontaneity combines with the resources available to the client. / Patchworkdesign integriert die Ressourcen des Auftraggebers, wie zum Beispiel Zeit, alte Möbel, Geld, in den Entwurf und die Umsetzung. Gestalterische Spontanität verbindet sich mit den dem jeweiligen Kunden zur Verfügung stehenden Mitteln.

Suggestions to young people. To young people he suggests to experiment much and to "have big eyes". One must consider what to do with his (her) time, "what's important and what isn't." "You have to deal with resources and time very carefully". As a company owner you have to grow with what you design. If he were to start over from the beginning once again, he would "attend the HTL[3], take the secondary school *Matura*[4] exam and study", because such a technical, specializing education also forms you as a human being.

---

3   The Höhere Technische Lehranstalt in Austria is a profession-oriented upper secondary school which is completed with the *Matura* exam.

4   The *Matura* (*Abitur* in Germany) is the final secondary school examination upon which the school-leaving *Matura* certificate is awarded, which entitles to study at a university. (Tr. n.)

Ratschläge an die Jungen. Jungen Menschen empfiehlt er, viel zu experimentieren und „große Augen zu haben". Überlegen müsse man sich, was man mit seiner Zeit macht, „was ist wichtig und nicht wichtig". „Mit Ressourcen und Zeit muss man sehr sorgsam umgehen." Als Unternehmer müsse man mit dem, was man gestaltet, wachsen. Wenn er selbst noch einmal am Anfang stünde, würde er „die HTL[1] besuchen, die Matura ablegen und studieren", weil eine solche Fachschulung einen auch als Menschen ausbilde.

---

1   Die Höhere Technische Lehranstalt ist in Österreich eine Berufsbildende Höhere Schule und wird mit der Matura abgeschlossen.

Rund 2 (2016)
On behalf of / Im Auftrag von: Das Rund
Particularly pragmatic, detailed solutions in craftsmanship and industrial prefabrication are taken into account in design and realization. / Bei Entwurf- und Umsetzung wurden insbesondere pragmatische Detaillösungen im Handwerk und die industrielle Vorfertigung berücksichtigt.

Wood / Holz

„Der Rohstoff Holz gibt
 Geborgenheit und
 vermittelt Wärme."
Martin Aigner

Martin Aigner

Beer table for Ottakringer / Biertisch für Ottakringer (2016)
On behalf of / Im Auftrag von: Ottakringer
Table for having fun with a rotating beer barrel in the middle. /
Tisch zum Spaßhaben mit drehbarem Bierfass in der Mitte.

Wood / Holz

Caroussel (2014)
On behalf of / Im Auftrag von: Carrousel Kids

Children's boutique with a mobile counter on tractor tyres and wooden funnels that serve as reflectors, among others. / Kinderboutique, unter anderem mit auf Traktorreifen fahrbarem Ladentisch und Holztrichtern, die als Reflektoren dienen.

Martin Aigner

Organic process-oriented work / Organisch Prozessorientiertes Arbeiten (2013)
On behalf of / Im Auftrag von: Various / Eigenentwicklung
A rough master plan is developed together with the commissioner of the work.
The Handgedacht team builds on site, trusting his creative feel for the space. /
Gemeinsam mit dem Auftraggeber wird ein grober Masterplan entwickelt.
Das Team von „Handgedacht" baut dann vor Ort und vertraut dabei seinem
gestalterischen Gefühl für den Platz.

Martin Aigner   1981 Born / Geb. in Bruck/Mur · 1997–2000: Carpentry apprenticeship at the carpentry company of Peter Greiner, Veitsch / Tischlerlehre Tischlereibetrieb Greiner Peter, Veitsch · 2001–2005: Journeyman and production manager at the carpentry company & socioeconomic enterprise Wohnwerkstatt, Bruck/Mur / Geselle und Fertigungsleiter im Tischlereibetrieb & SÖB Wohnwerkstatt, Bruck/Mur · 2005–2007: Freelance carpenter while taking a master course at WIFI, Graz / Selbstständiger Tischler, parallel Meisterkurs am WIFI, Graz · 2007–2011: Studied interior design at the New Design University St. Pölten / Studium Innenarchitektur an der New Design University St. Pölten · 2012–2015: Freelance carpenter and designer for MAAI / Selbstständig als Tischler und Designer unter MAAI · 2015: Founded his own company Handgedacht / Gründung des eigenen Betriebs Handgedacht

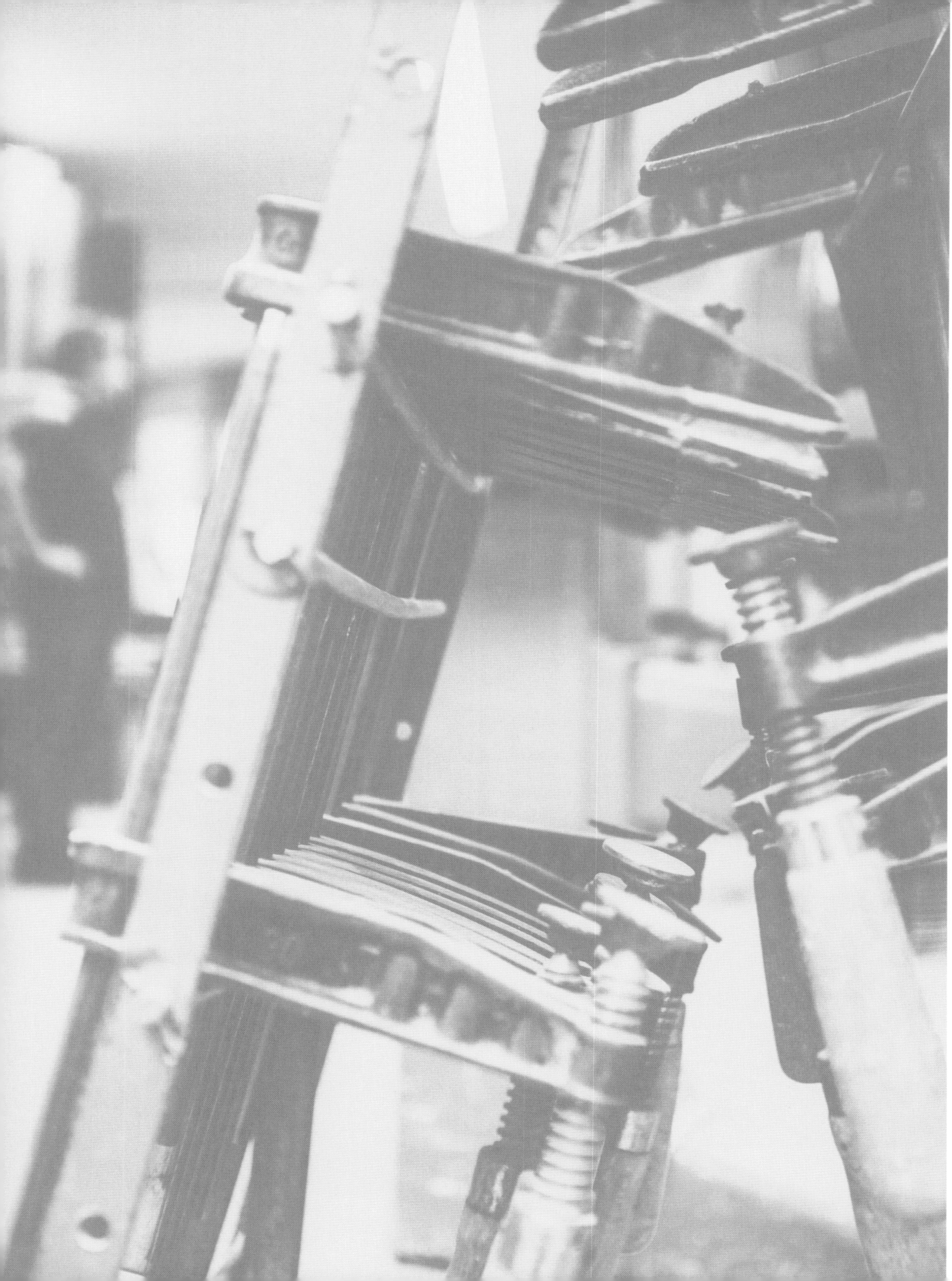

Wood is a special material. And the love for it is even more so, once you have discovered it. First the usual educational path, the notorious Austrian schools, military service, then joiner including the master joiner exam and the taking over of a company. In the third section of life, so to say as retired. But without silence. The pipes are not of wood, of course, but almost everything else of an organ which the wood specialist—who knows exactly that mostly only the alloy or the combined effect of materials produces the wonder—has been able to operate since he was ten years old.

Holz ist ein besonderer Stoff. Und die Liebe zu ihm noch besonderer, wenn man sie entdeckt hat. Zuerst der übliche Weg, die notorischen österreichischen Schulen einschließlich Bundesheer, dann Tischler samt Meisterprüfung und Betriebsübernahme. Im dritten Lebensabschnitt sozusagen im Ruhestand. Aber ohne Stille. Die Pfeifen sind freilich nicht aus Holz, aber fast alles andere einer Orgel, die der Holzfachmann, der genau weiß, dass meist erst die Legierung oder das Zusammenwirken von Stoffen das Wunder ergibt, seit seinem elften Lebensjahr bedienen kann.

Wood / Holz

There's nothing like starting young. The very first master teacher was the father, who put the five-year-old boy on the joiner's bench and let him make the earliest experiences. The actual apprenticeship with and on the side of his father, however, was no children's game. Today a hole in the workshop door is the proof of who was the boss, namely the one who threw the plane at the apprentice boy, without catching him. Now the master, as he was to become, smiles when he remembers the father's anger and the throw.

Früh übt sich, wer ein Meister wird. Der allererste Lehrherr war der Vater, der den Fünfjährigen auf die Hobelbank gesetzt und ihn die frühesten Erfahrungen hat machen lassen. Die tatsächliche Lehre mit und neben dem Vater war jedoch kein Kinderspiel. Ein Loch in der Werkstatttür legt heute Zeugnis davon ab, wer der Chef war, nämlich jener, der den Hobel nach dem Lehrbuben geworfen hat, ... ohne ihn zu treffen. Nun schmunzelt der nachmalige Meister, wenn er sich an die Wut des Vaters und den Wurf erinnert.

The master's favorite wood. The way was predetermined, for a business had to be taken over. The master certificate was absolutely necessary. And in Tyrol there was plenty of material. Mainly stone pine. "Solid only, of course". For example, as bed with a medical effect alike, "because while sleeping the heart rhythm can be lowered due to the ethereal smell of resin." He's also taken with spruce wood containing resin. With this wood "you can work beautifully" and give it a fine polish.

Das Lieblingsholz des Meisters. Der Weg war vorgezeichnet, zumal ein Betrieb zu übernehmen war. Der Meister(brief) war unabdingbar. Und Material war in Tirol genug vorhanden. Vor allem Zirbenholz. „Natürlich nur massiv." Zum Beispiel als Bett mit gleichsam medizinischer Wirkung, „weil der Herzrhythmus im Schlaf wegen des ätherischen Harzgeruchs gesenkt werden kann." Auch das Fichtenholz mit Harzgehalt hat es ihm angetan. Mit diesem Holz „kann man schön arbeiten" und ihm einen Feinschliff verpassen.

"The succession in the third generation is ensured."
Arnold Meusburger

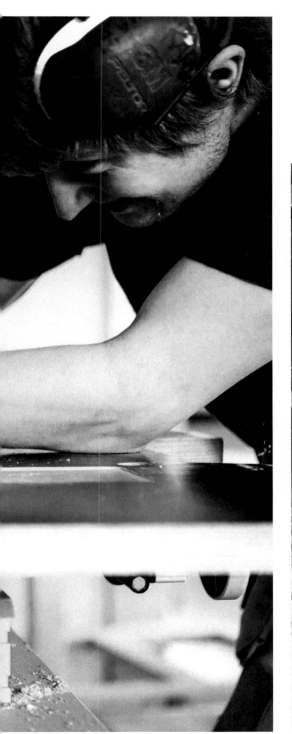

Old wood and young architects. When he realizes, in 1986, that you may (re)use old wood from houses which are being torn down and razed to the ground, "for me this was an issue". (Today, thirty years later, this utilization is booming.) In the Bregenz forest he personally triggered off the recycling, despite the fact that at the beginning people smiled at him. He had to smile himself, though about the architects who had just come out from university, who planned complete hotel furniture, "but lacked any experience whatsoever".

Great customers are modest. He had exciting experiences with customers who were from outside of Tyrol, in Liechtenstein or in Switzerland. "I've had seventy percent of my customers from Switzerland." He has refused assignments whenever there wasn't enough

Altholz und Jungarchitekten. Als er, und zwar im Jahr 1986, erkennt, dass man das Altholz aus Häusern, die abgebrochen und geschliffen werden, (wieder)verwenden könnte, „war das ein Punkt für mich". (Heute, dreißig Jahre später, ist diese Nutzbarmachung ein Boom.) Im Bregenzer Wald habe er persönlich das Recycling ausgelöst, obwohl man ihn zunächst belächelt habe. Er selber musste über die Architekten schmunzeln, die gerade von der Universität gekommen sind, komplette Hoteleinrichtungen geplant hätten, „aber vorne und hinten ohne Erfahrung" gewesen seien.

Tolle Kunden sind bescheiden. Spannende Geschichten habe er mit Kunden erlebt, die außerhalb Tirols beheimatet waren, in Liechtenstein oder der Schweiz. „Ich habe siebzig Prozent der Kunden in der Schweiz ge-

„Die Nachfolge in dritter Generation ist gesichert."
Arnold Meusburger

Armada Mobile (1999)
On behalf of / Im Auftrag von: Self-commissioned / Eigenauftrag
Mobile high gloss furniture in different colors that can be arranged individually. / Mobile Hochglanzmöbel, in unterschiedlichen Farben individuell zusammenstellbar.

Mobile humidor / Fahrbarer Humidor (unknown / unbekannt)
On behalf of / Im Auftrag von: Private / Privat
Humidor of massive cherrywood, oiled. Trays of cedar wood. /
Humidor aus Kirsche massiv, geölt. Einsätze aus Zedernholz.

understanding with the customer. At the handing over of the enterprise his father even suggested to him for which professional group he should not work. He sensed on the phone already if there could be an understanding with a prospective customer, or not. Essentially, he was enthusiastic too soon, as his wife remarks. A great order, the first one with old wood, was a complete home furniture for Germans in Tyrol, which reminded him of Felix Mitterer's "Piefke[1]-Saga".

The machine-made dovetails. The craft has changed due to engineering. A CNC-programmed machine works "more perfectly", by hand you never get that degree of perfection and "manually you couldn't make dovetails that beautiful." Quality has improved and the price has

habt." Er habe Arbeiten abgelehnt, wenn er mit Auftraggebern nicht habe können. Bei der Betriebsübergabe habe ihm sein Vater sogar geraten, für welchen Berufsstand er nicht arbeiten solle. Er habe schon am Telefon erkannt, ob er mit einem Kunden können werde oder nicht. Im Grund habe er sich immer zu schnell begeistert, wie seine Ehefrau meint. Ein schöner Auftrag, der erste mit Altholz, sei eine komplette Hauseinrichtung für Deutsche in Tirol gewesen, was ihn an Felix Mitterers „Piefke-Saga" erinnert habe.

Die maschinellen Schwalbenschwanzzinken. Das Handwerk habe sich durch die Technik verändert. Eine Maschine mit CNC-Programm arbeite „perfekter", „mit der Hand werde es nie so sauber" und könne man

1   Denigratory term used by Austrians meaning Germans. (Tr. n.)

gone down. Creativity still allows to score, though. He draws his designs by hand. In that he has to comply with rules, of course. "A bench can't simply be fifty high, it's got to be forty six high." Centimeters, naturally.

The ensured succession. From today's view he wouldn't do anything different. "I enjoy what happens." He already has a successor. To him he gives good suggestions, the same way he received those from his father. "Keep it simple, and whenever it's possible don't get dependent on architects. Work with good architects. One hundred percent. But don't get dependent."

"händisch Schwalbenschwanzzinken gar nicht so schön machen". Die Qualität habe sich erhöht und der Preis verringert. Punkten könne man noch mit Kreativität. Er zeichne seine Entwürfe mit der Hand. Natürlich müsse er sich dabei an Regeln halten. „Eine Bank kann nicht einfach fünfzig hoch sein, sie muss sechsundvierzig hoch sein." Naturgemäß Zentimeter.

Die gesicherte Nachfolge. Aus heutiger Sicht würde er nichts anders machen. „Ich habe eine Freude mit dem, was passiert." Einen Nachfolger habe er schon. Dem er gute Ratschläge erteilt, wie er sie von seinem Vater bekommen habe. „Einfach und wenn möglich, nicht von den Architekten abhängig werden. Mit guten Architekten zusammenarbeiten. Zu einhundert Prozent. Aber nicht abhängig werden."

Habitation and customization work / Wohnen und Anpassarbeiten (2016)
On behalf of / Im Auftrag von: Self-commissioned / Eigenauftrag
Generous renovation of a flat including a panoramic view. Customization of his workshop in Bizau. / Großzügiger Wohnungsausbau mit Rundumsicht inklusive Anpassarbeiten am eigenen Werkstattgebäude in Bizau.

The self-supporting circle /
Der selbsttragende Kreis
(2000)

The self-supporting circle / Der selbsttragende Kreis (2000)
On behalf of / Im Auftrag von: Self-commissioned / Eigenauftrag
Maple wood kit that playfully brings giving and taking into harmony. /
Holzbausatz aus Ahorn, der Geben und Nehmen spielerisch in
Einklang bringen soll.

Arnold Meusburger

Old building restoration / Althaussanierung (2003)
On behalf of / Im Auftrag von: Maritha & Martin Waldner
Renovation of a house built in 1782 in conjunction with new architecture.
Wooden walls and old structures were uncovered. / Umbau eines
Hauses aus dem Jahr 1782 in Verbindung mit neuer Architektur. Dabei
wurden Strickwände und alte Strukturen sichtbar gemacht.

Arnold Meusburger

Kitchen installation / Küchenverbau (2011)
On behalf of / Im Auftrag von: Anonymous / Anonym
Kitchen installation in massive silver fir, oiled. /
Küchenverbau in Weißtanne massiv, geölt.

Arnold Meusburger   1950 Born / Geb. in Bizau • 1965–1968: Carpentry apprenticeship at the carpentry company of Georg Meusburger, Bizau / Tischlerlehre im Tischlereibetrieb Georg Meusburger, Bizau • 1971: Master craftsman exam / Meisterprüfung • 1975: Took over the company from Georg Meusburger, Bizau. Self-employed until retirement in 2011. / Übernahme des Betriebs von Georg Meusburger, Bizau. Selbstständig bis zur Pensionierung 2011

She grew up with wool. In a textile city in northern Germany. Wool bobbles on the streets. Acid smell in the air. Strong metal rhythms behind the windows of big brick buildings. Looms in action. As strongest childhood impressions. Resulting from all that, studies of textile design, interior design[1] and textile restor-ation. And eventually, three decades ago, establishing of her own textile atelier in Vienna, where she works as an artist, too. For exhibitions and orders in and from Brazil, China, Europe and the United States of America.

Groß geworden sei sie mit Wolle. In einer Textilstadt im Norden Deutschlands. Wollflusen auf den Straßen. Säuerlicher Geruch in der Luft. Starke metallische Rhythmen hinter großen Backstein-gebäudefenstern. Webstühle in Aktion. Als stärkste Eindrücke der Kindheit. Daraus folgend Studien des Textildesigns, der Innen-architektur und Textilrestaurierung. Und schließlich vor drei Jahr-zehnten die Gründung eines eigenen Textilateliers in Wien, in dem sie arbeite und künstlerisch tätig sei. Für Ausstellungen und Aufträge in und aus Brasilien, China, Europa und den Vereinigten Staaten von Amerika.

1 Literally translated "indoor architecture." (Tr. n.)

Beate von Harten

Textiles / Textil

The smell of wool. When she went to the music lessons as a small child in her hometown Neumünster, she heard the noises of the loom, its rhythm. She kept asking herself what melody that was. She received the elucidation to that at the age of nineteen, when she completed an internship in the factory. "Then I understood what these machines were telling". She saw the shuttle, which in its back and forth movement produced the wool bobbles. "Then the smell of wool was also there." The components had assembled. All the way to the study of fashion and textile design as well as interior

Der Geruch der Wolle. Als sie, das Kind, zum Musikunterricht in ihrer Heimatstadt Neumünster gegangen sei, habe sie die Geräusche des Webstuhls, seinen Rhythmus, gehört. Sie habe sich immer gefragt, welche Melodie dies sei. Aufklärung habe sie erfahren, als sie mit neunzehn Jahren ein Praktikum in der Fabrik absolviert habe. „Dann habe ich verstanden, was diese Geräte erzählt haben." Sie habe das Schiffchen gesehen, das im Hin- und Herfahren Wollflusen erzeugt habe. „Der Geruch der Wolle war dann auch da." Die Komponenten hätten sich zusammengefügt. Bis zu den Studien aus

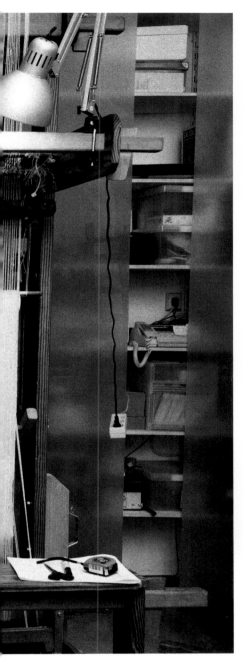

design. With a very good craft education because of the weaving projects.

The carpet weaving mill apprentice. She still profits today from the excellent education received in the study. "Yes, from all that opportunity to experiment, and to really do things on a high level, with beautiful and expensive materials." Next to school and study she received instruction in piano and organ and passed an exam in organ. Later she became her own apprentice and taught herself carpet weaving.

Mode- und Textildesign sowie Innenarchitektur. Mit sehr guter handwerklicher Ausbildung wegen der Webprojekte.

Der Teppichwebereilehrling. Von der ausgezeichneten Ausbildung im Studium zehre sie heute noch. „Ja, von dieser ganzen Möglichkeit zu experimentieren und wirklich auf einem hohen Niveau Dinge zu machen mit schönen und teuren Materialien." Neben Schule und Studium habe sie Klavier- und Orgelunterricht erhalten und eine Orgelprüfung bestanden. Später sei sie ihr eigener Lehrling gewesen und habe sich die Teppich- weberei beigebracht.

The finishing of the material. She works with linen, silk and wool. If she had the time, for her it would be interesting to experiment with bamboo and other fibers. "Of course I love silk and I love that shine." She is attracted by the varied colors of the material, by the bluntness of wool and the varied surfaces. And by the noble quality of silk. "When I weave tapestry I use silk and gold and silver, and wool also." She uses pure natural colors. For a long time she has been showing consideration for the "use of animals."

Die Veredelung des Materials. Sie arbeite mit Leinen, Seide und Wolle. Hätte sie die Zeit, wäre es für sie interessant mit Bambus und anderen Fasern zu experimentieren. „Ich liebe natürlich Seide und ich liebe diesen Glanz." Die unterschiedliche Farbigkeit des Materials, die Stumpfheit der Wolle und die verschiedenen Oberflächen sprechen sie an. Und das Edle der Seide. „Wenn ich eine Tapisserie webe, greife ich auf Seide und Gold und Silber zurück und auch Wolle." Sie verwende reine Naturfarben. Seit Langem nehme sie Rücksicht auf die „Tierbenutzung".

Her noble motto is:
"Slow art for a fast time."
Beate von Harten

Sand, 95×275 cm (2014/2015)
On behalf of / Im Auftrag von: Andrea Koppensteiner
Linen carpet as requested by the client. /
Leinenteppich nach Kundenwunsch.

Textiles / Textil

left / links: Future, 160×220 cm (2014/2015)
On behalf of / Im Auftrag von: Self-commissioned / Eigenauftrag
Subdued color landscape, painterly abstract with a positive ecological footprint – woven in pure linen, subtly mixed colours. /
Sanfte Farblandschaft – malerisch abstrakt mit positivem ökologischem Fußabdruck. Gewebt in reinem Leinen, farblich subtil gemischt.

Beate von Harten

Caucasus / Kaukasus, 64×170 cm (2014)
On behalf of / Im Auftrag von: Self-commissioned / Eigenauftrag
Tapestry, wool and silk woven on a high warp loom in about 400 hours. /
Tapisserie, Wolle und Seide in ca. 400 Stunden am Hochwebstuhl gewebt.

The professions with freshness and boldness. On one hand she manufactures "textiles for the room". Tapestries and carpets. On the other hand she restores them. Kilims, tapestries, valuable oriental carpets as well as silk embroidery. "I have two professions. What I care about is freshness. Impudence is important to me. I care about boldness." Of course she also has problematic customers "and the opposite, appreciating ones, with whom you can have great conversations and who almost hang on my every word".

Die Berufe mit Frische und Kühnheit. Einerseits stelle sie „Textilien für den Raum" her. Tapisserien und Teppiche. Andererseits restauriere sie. Kelims, Tapisserien, kostbare orientalische Teppiche sowie Seidenstickereien. „Ich habe zwei Berufe. Es geht mir um Frische. Es geht mir um Frechheit. Es geht mir um Kühnheit." Sie habe natürlich auch problematische Kunden „und das Gegenteil, wertschätzende, mit denen man sehr schöne Gespräche führen kann und die mir fast an den Lippen hängen".

The weave of threads, light ropes and metal. The "Planets", a tapestry, "was a very important work" for her, and "two linen carpets". On the "Planets" she worked for months. In her creations she is "totally open" towards the new technologies. She finds very exciting what is being created now. She would like to try her hand once at "threads, lights, light ropes" and metal.

Das Gewebe aus Fäden, Lichtsträngen und Metall. Die „Planeten", eine Tapisserie, seien für sie „eine ganz wichtige Arbeit gewesen" und „zwei Leinenteppiche". An den „Planeten" habe sie über Monate gearbeitet. In ihrem Schaffen sei sie für die neuen Technologien „total offen". Sie finde „sehr spannend", was jetzt entstehe. Gern würde sie sich einmal an „Fäden, Leuchten, Lichtsträngen" und Metall versuchen.

Ihr edles Motto lautet:
„Langsame Kunst für
eine schnelle Zeit."
Beate von Harten

The feeling for the material. To young designers she is able "to give along a whole lot, my enthusiasm and fascination for textile arts." She conveys her knowledge, she cooperates. She is able to give to them her "feelings for the material and the view of aesthetics." She is able to "make them aware about all that combination of history, material, technique and so on". Maybe her daughter, with whom she works, will lead the enterprise into the next generation.

Das Gefühl für das Material. Jungen Gestalterinnen und Gestaltern könne sie „unheimlich viel mitgeben, meine Begeisterung und Faszination für die Textilkunst". Sie vermittle ihr Wissen, sie kooperiere. Sie könne ihnen ihre „Gefühle für das Material und die Sichtweise zur Ästhetik mitgeben". Sie könne ihnen „diese ganze Kombination aus Geschichte, Material, Technik und so weiter bewusst machen". Vielleicht werde die Tochter, mit der sie zusammenarbeite, den Betrieb in die nächste Generation führen.

Commissioned work / Auftragsarbeit (2016/2017)
On behalf of / Im Auftrag von: Hans Schneider, Clarissa Lindner
Three linen carpets woven into curved shapes. Made of a pure linen weft, a pure wool warp and white silk as requested by the commissioner. / Drei Leinenteppiche teilweise in Kurvenform gewebt. Hergestellt aus reinem Leinen im Schuss, reiner Wolle in der Kette und weißer Seide auf Wunsch des Auftraggebers.

Chosrau's Spring – Reloaded
(1999–2002)

Beate von Harten

Chosrau's Spring – Reloaded, 160×180 cm (2016)
On behalf of / Im Auftrag von: Self-commissioned / Eigenauftrag
Wool, silk, gold, gems and beads woven on a high warp loom in European tapestry technique and combined with macramé. / Wolle, Seide, Gold, Edelsteine und Perlen in europäischer Tapisserietechnik auf dem Hochwebstuhl gewebt und mit orientalischer Knüpftechnik vereint.

Beate von Harten   1953 Born / Geb. in Neumünster, Germany / Deutschland · 1973–1978: Studied fashion and textile design at the University of Applied Sciences in Hamburg / Studium Mode und Textildesign an der Fachhochschule Hamburg · 1981–1982: Studied interior design at the State Academy of Fine Arts in Stuttgart / Studium Innenarchitektur an der Staatlichen Akademie der Bildenden Künste in Stuttgart · 1982–1984: Textile restoration at Rippon Boswell, Kensington, London / Textilrestaurierung bei Rippon Boswell, Kensington, London · 1984: Started freelance work in her own textile atelier in Vienna / Beginn der Selbstständigkeit mit eigenem Textil-Atelier in Wien

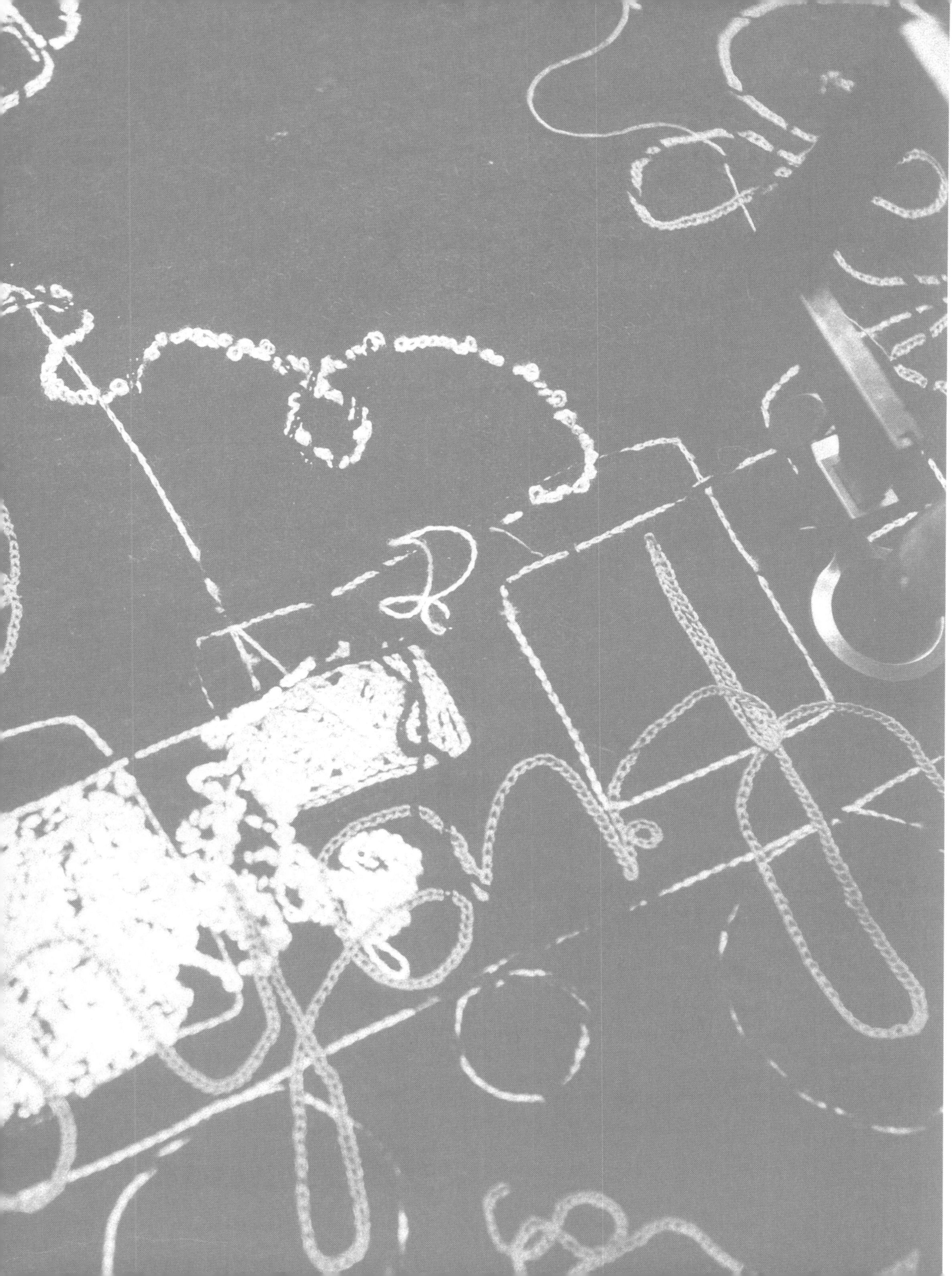

Her material is textiles, all her life. They weave her biography, her craft, her art. In approximately two decades of a comprehensive activity the result of the weave is not a multicolored carpet, but a diverse one (one made of experiences). With exhibitions and cooperations and art projects. As well as many instruction experiences made in adult education. The geography of her activity reaches from Vienna or Haslach in Upper Austria all the way to Montreal and Ottawa in Canada as well as China, Germany and Spain.

Ihr Stoff sind ein Leben lang die Textilien. Sie weben ihre Biografie, ihr Handwerk, ihre Kunst. Das Gewebe ergibt in ungefähr zwei Jahrzehnten umfangreicher Tätigkeit keinen bunten, sondern einen vielfältigen (Erfahrungs-)Teppich. Mit Ausstellungen und Kooperationen und Kunstprojekten. Sowie vielen Unterrichtserlebnissen in der Erwachsenenbildung. Die Geografie ihrer Tätigkeit reicht dabei von Wien oder Haslach in Oberösterreich bis Montreal und Ottawa in Kanada sowie China, Deutschland und Spanien.

A *Matura* exam made of gold and pearls. In 1996 she took the *Matura* and the journey-woman exams at the HBLA[1] in Vienna, Hasnerstrasse. Focus subjects were gold and pearl embroidery. She came into contact with her craft for the first time at school. "In 1996, in the 'Kolleg' in Spengergasse, Vienna", where she graduated with a diploma. From the "legal point of view" first she was a machine embroideress. With a business license which she has returned in the meantime. Today she is a freelance artist with an individually owned enterprise. She set up her own business.

Eine Matura aus Gold und Perlen. Die Matura und Gesellenprüfung habe sie im Jahr 1996 an der HBLA[1] in Wien, Hasnerstraße, abgelegt. Aus den Fächern Gold- und Perlenstickerei. Mit ihrem Handwerk sei sie zum ersten Mal in der Schule in Berührung gekommen. „1996 im Kolleg in der Wiener Spengergasse", das sie mit einem Diplom absolviert habe. Aus „rechtlicher Sicht" sei sie zunächst Maschinenstickerin gewesen. Mit Gewerbeschein, den sie inzwischen zurückgelegt habe. Heute sei sie freischaffende Künstlerin mit einem Einzelunternehmen. Sie habe sich selbstständig gemacht.

1   The Höhere Bundeslehranstalt in Austria is a profession-oriented upper secondary school which is completed with the *Matura* exam.

1   Die Höhere Bundeslehranstalt ist in Österreich eine Berufsbildende Höhere Schule und wird mit der Matura abgeschlossen.

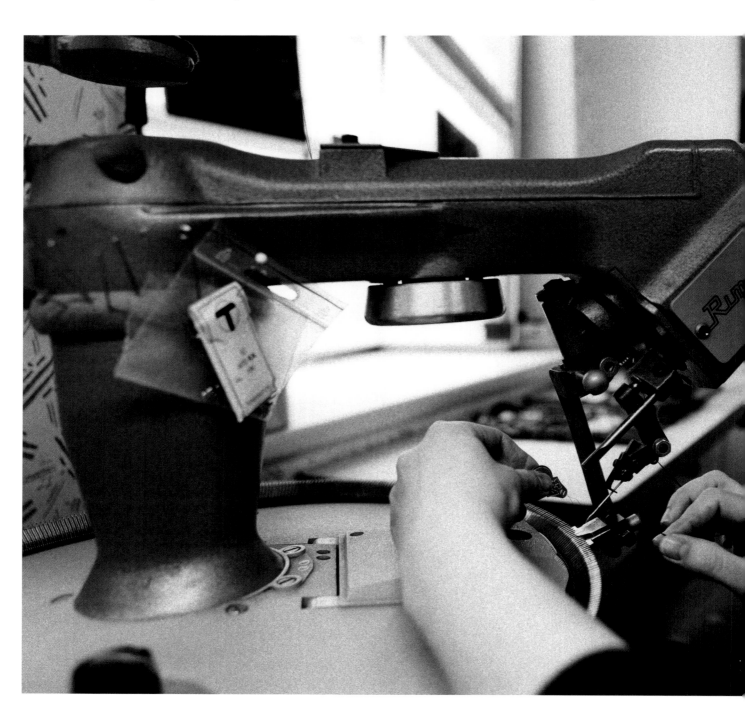

At the interface between design and craft. Design-wise at school she didn't learn that much. Regarding engineering, though, "a whole lot" was offered, and she still "profits" from that today for her work. It was a type of knowledge which bears the risk that it gets lost. Later in Canada for three months she attended a technical specializing textile school in Montreal. There the "instruction was right at the interface between craft and design, within a small framework". With all the necessary spinning machines and power looms. To her young colleagues she warmly suggests to do stays abroad.

An der Schnittstelle zwischen Design und Handwerk. Gestalterisch habe sie in der Schule weniger gelernt. Im Technischen sei aber „enorm viel geboten" worden, was ihr noch heute für die Arbeit „viel bringt". Es sei ein Wissen gewesen, bei dem die Gefahr bestehe, dass es sich verliert. Später habe sie in Kanada drei Monate lang eine textile Fachhochschule in Montreal besucht. Dort sei genau „an der Schnittstelle zwischen Handwerk und Design in kleinem Rahmen unterrichtet" worden. Mit allen erforderlichen Spinn- und Webmaschinen. Jungen Kolleginnen und Kollegen würde sie Auslandsaufenthalte besonders ans Herz legen.

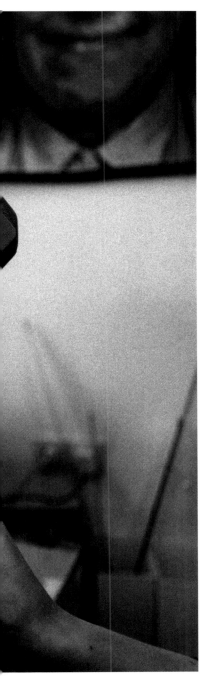

"Now it's totally popular that everything looks handmade."
Veronika Perché

„Jetzt ist es total beliebt,
dass alles handgemacht
ausschaut."

Veronika Perché

Fukushima (2015)
On behalf of / Im Auftrag von: Laura Schreiner
Knitted fabric to cover two stools with a motif of the reactor
blocks in Fukushima, Japan. / Strickstoff für die Bespannung zweier
Hocker nach dem Motiv der Reaktorblöcke in Fukushima, Japan.

Experiments with steel wire. She works with thread as well as (merino) wool and she experiments with nylon, paper yarn and steel wire. It's an issue "from where do I get in Austria industrial threads. The textile industry has shrunk a lot, unfortunately." She doesn't need large quantities, either. A pulloverweighs less than half a kilogram. Unfortunately, there are only a few companies "which deal with such small quantities." She produces "much clothing, which has to be kind to the skin and rather easy to handle". Sometimes she is being asked whether instead of animal wool there is also some vegan substitute material. There isn't, and synthetic fibers made of poly-acryl "today are a no-go."

Experimente mit Stahldraht. Sie arbeite mit Garn sowie (Merino-)Wolle und experimentiere mit Nylon, Papiergarn und Stahldraht. Es sei eine Frage, „woher bekomme ich in Österreich Industriegarne. Die Textilindustrie ist ja leider sehr geschrumpft." Sie brauche auch keine großen Mengen. Ein Pullover wiege weniger als ein halbes Kilogramm. Leider gäbe es wenig Firmen, „die mit so kleinen Mengen handeln". Sie produziere „viel Bekleidung, die hautfreundlich und halbwegs pflegeleicht sein muss". Manchmal werde sie gefragt, ob es statt der tierischen Wolle auch veganes Ersatzmaterial gebe. Gebe es nicht, und synthetische Fasern aus Polyacryl seien „heutzutag ein No-Go".

left / links: Ute Bock (2010)
right / rechts: Rosie (2011)
On behalf of / Im Auftrag von: Self-commissioned / Eigenauftrag
"Ute Bock" knitted portrait. "Rosie" arose to mark 100 years of the
women's movement in Austria. „Ute Bock" Trikografie. „Rosie"
entstand anlässlich „100 Jahre Frauenbewegung in Österreich".

Trikografie
(2010–2011)

Shape and cut design. "Most orders I get are clothing, apparel." Earlier she worked only for fashion designers according to their designs. "Actually, that was just fashion, fashion, fashion. That bothered me." Now next to that she works in the area of costumes. For example, she has made bathing suits from the 1910s and 1920s. She doesn't make any designs, "shape and cut pattern design" are set by the customers, by those placing the orders. Generally speaking, she is active wherever "you can use textile". As a "one-woman business" naturally she is not able to accept too large orders.

Form und Schnittgestaltung. „Die meisten Aufträge, die ich habe, betreffen Bekleidung." Früher hätte sie bloß für Modedesigner nach deren Entwürfen gearbeitet. „Das war eigentlich nur Mode, Mode, Mode. Das hat mich gestört." Jetzt werke sie daneben im Kostümbereich. Beispielsweise habe sie Badeanzüge aus den Zehner- und Zwanzigerjahren des vorigen Jahrhunderts hergestellt. Entwürfe mache sie keine, „Form und Schnittgestaltung" werde von den Auftraggebern vorgegeben. Insgesamt sei sie überall dort tätig, „wo man Textil einsetzen kann". Zu große Aufträge könne sie als „Ein-Frau-Betrieb" naturgemäß nicht annehmen.

Veronika Persché

Vision 4/2 (2016–2017)
On behalf of / Im Auftrag von: Mads Dinesen
Pullover and scarf with motif and lettering for the collection Vision 4/2
by Mads Dinesen. / Pullover und Schal mit Motiv und Schriftzug für die
Kollektion Vision 4/2 von Mads Dinesen.

Exceptional artists confirm the rule. As customers she has artists, those who have made it and young ones, but also non-artists. Her experience is that creative people can be uncomplicated. "Logically it is more pleasant to work with professionals." She has no reservations against new technologies. The knitting development is evidently going towards on-demand production. Very important works are her knit portrait of Ute Bock, "which I have produced on a machine", and the "We Can Do It" motif of the American women's movement, which she has knit for the one hundredth women's day in Austria in 2011.

Ausnahmekünstler bestätigen die Regel. Als KundInnen habe sie KünstlerInnen, arrivierte und junge, aber auch NichtkünstlerInnen. Ihre Erfahrung sei, dass Kreative unkompliziert sein können. „Logischerweise ist es angenehmer, mit Profis zu arbeiten." Gegen neue Technologien habe sie keine Vorbehalte. Die Strickentwicklung gehe offensichtlich in die Richtung der On-Demand-Produktion. Sehr wichtige Werke seien ihr Ute-Bock-Strickportrait, „das ich auf einer Maschine produziert habe", und das Motiv „We Can Do It" der amerikanischen Frauenbewegung, das sie für den einhundertsten Frauentag in Österreich im Jahr 2011 gestrickt habe.

Merino wool in design:context (2011)
On behalf of / Im Auftrag von: Miki Martinek
Series of knitted stools, cushions and blankets in cooperation with Miki Martinek. / Serie von Strickhockern, Kissen und Decken in Zusammenarbeit mit Miki Martinek.

Veronika Persché

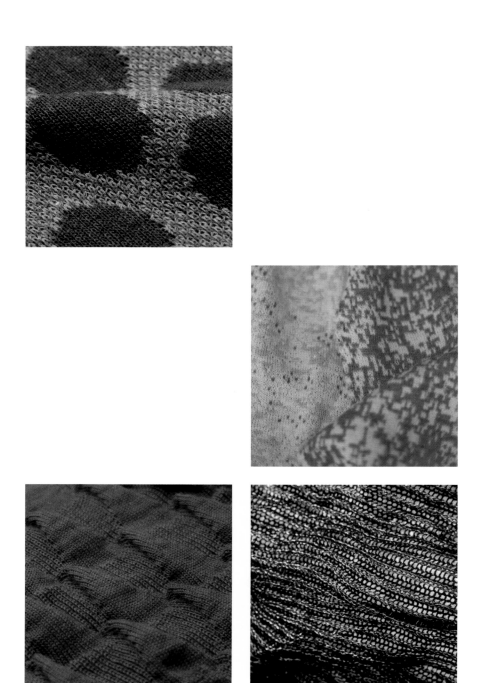

Knitted fabric designs / Strickstoff Designs (2010–2017)
On behalf of / Im Auftrag von: Artist's collection / Eigene Kollektion
Reversible jacquard knit of recycled yarn, organic cotton and merino wool.
Three-dimensional fabric of lambswool. Experimental fabric design of
merino wool and steel wire. / Doppelseitig verwendbarer Jacquardstrick aus
Recyclinggarn, Bio-Baumwolle und Merinowolle. Dreidimensionaler Stoff
aus Schurwolle. Experimentelles Stoffdesign aus Merinowolle und Stahldraht.

Veronika Persché   1976 Born / Geb. in Klosterneuburg • 1991–1996: HBLA in Herbststraße, 16th district, Vienna / HBLA in Wien 16,
Herbststraße • 1996: School-leaving certificate, apprenticeship certification exam for goldwork and beadwork embroidery / Matura,
Gesellenprüfung für Gold- und Perlenstickerei • 1996–1998: College for Textile Design, HTBLVA in Spengergasse, 5th district, Vienna /
Kolleg für Textildesign, HTBLVA in Wien 5, Spengergasse • 2001: Started freelance work / Beginn der Selbstständigkeit • 2010: Guest
artist at CTCM Montreal, Canada / Gastkünstlerin am CTCM Montreal, Kanada

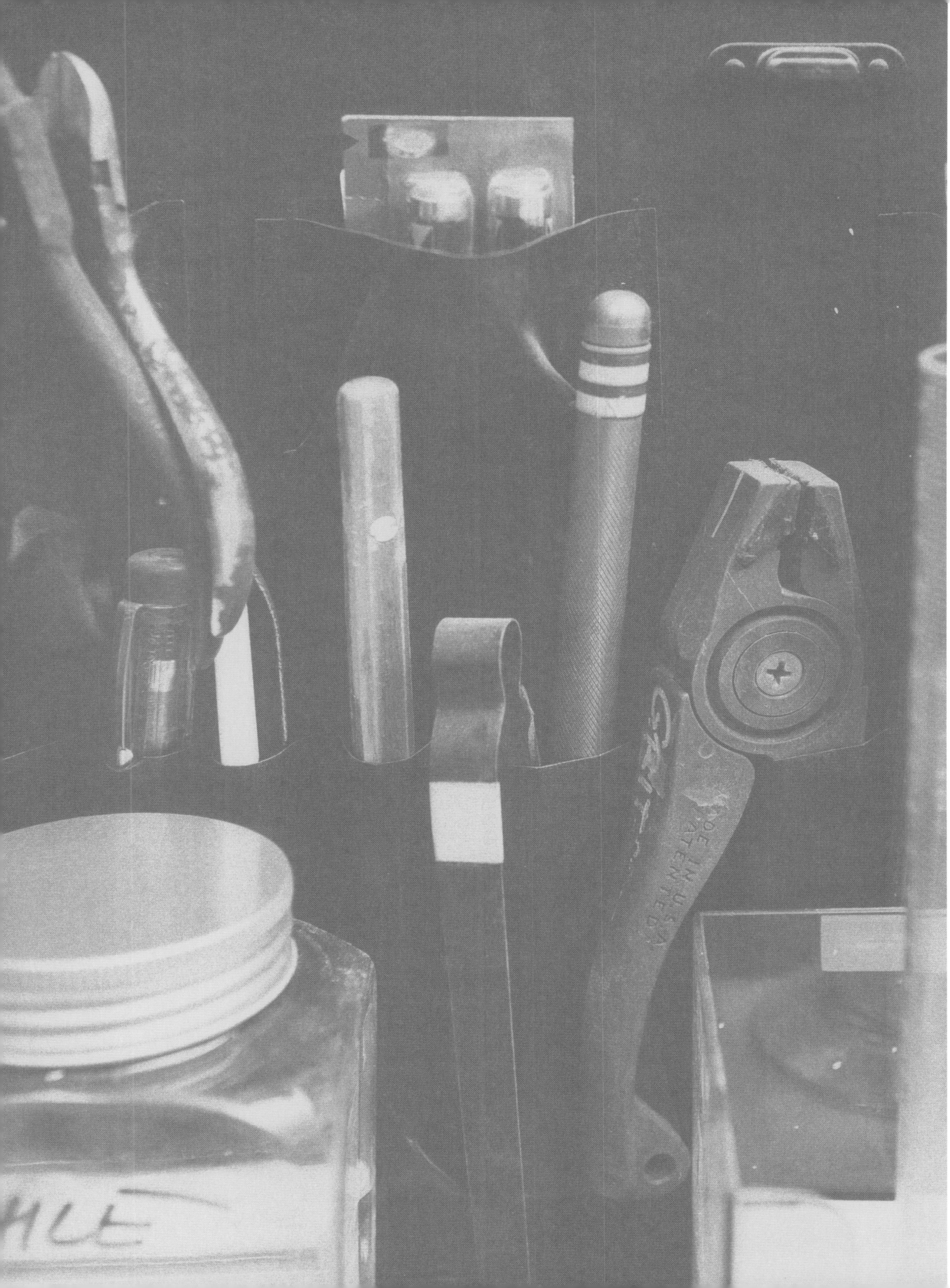

Luck in this case is made of glass. One's whole life. He interrupted gymnasium one year before the end. Nevertheless, he became a teacher and an internationally sought-after lecturer in the field of glass design and glass fusing. In the famous Technical School for Glass Kramsach he passes the master exam. First he begins free-lance, he works also in the United States of America, and eventually he is a HTL[1] teacher for thirty years now. One may define his works with the adjectives profane and sacral as well as by the nouns art and craft.

Das Glück ist in diesem Fall aus Glas. Ein Leben lang. Das Gymnasium hat er ein Jahr vor dem Ende abgebrochen. Dennoch ist er Lehrer geworden und ein international gesuchter Vortragender in Sachen Glasgestaltung und Schmelzglas. In der berühmten Glasfachschule Kramsach legt er die Meisterprüfung ab, beginnt zuerst freischaffend, arbeitet auch in den Vereinigten Staaten von Amerika und ist schließlich seit dreißig Jahren HTL[1]-Lehrer. Seine Arbeiten kann man mit den Adjektiven profan und sakral sowie den Nomen Kunst und Kunsthandwerk bestimmen.

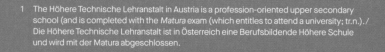

1   The Höhere Technische Lehranstalt in Austria is a profession-oriented upper secondary school (and is completed with the *Matura* exam (which entitles to attend a university; t.r.n.)./ Die Höhere Technische Lehranstalt ist in Österreich eine Berufsbildende Höhere Schule und wird mit der Matura abgeschlossen.

Rudolf Gritsch

Glass / Glas

The walk to school becomes his fate. During his school years day by day he walks past an art glazier's workshop. The fence in front of the area is fitted with glass plates which fascinate him so much that he knows, "this is it". Upon inquiring about it, he can start the apprenticeship. "The period of my apprenticeship was the best in my life, because every day was a voyage of discovery." At the company restorations were done, but also "all-modern works". He admired his master because of his wide experience.

The stone-and-glass combination of sacral architecture. After six years he quits the company and later in a technical-vocational school he builds up the department of

Der Schulweg wird zum Schicksal. Während seiner Schulzeit geht er Tag für Tag an einer Kunstglaserei vorbei. Der Zaun vor dem Gelände ist mit Glasplatten versehen, die ihn so faszinieren, dass er weiß, „das ist es". Auf Nachfrage kann er mit der Lehre beginnen. „Die Lehrzeit war die schönste Zeit meines Lebens, da jeder Tag eine Entdeckungsreise war." In der Firma wurden Restaurierungen durchgeführt, aber auch „ganz moderne Arbeiten". Seinen Meister habe er wegen dessen großer Erfahrung bewundert.

Die Stein-Glas-Kombination der Sakralarchitektur. Nach sechs Jahren verlässt er den Betrieb und baut später in einer Fachschule die Abteilung für Schmelz-

glass fusing. He established his own company in order to make his own pictures and objects as well as sculptures, and sell them via galleries. As a result of this, contacts happened with persons for whom he had to co-design and execute works. In the meantime, for example, he has designed altars, windows and desks in seven churches. The customers with hand shake quality are the ones he prefers. With "contracts with thousand provisions" troubles are pre-programmed. Among the ordered works three churches are the most important projects, among them the Millennium Church. Artistically speaking, the "Swimming Stones" are the highlight.

glaserei auf. Den eigenen Betrieb gründete er, um seine Bilder, Objekte sowie Skulpturen anzufertigen und sie über Galerien zu verkaufen. Es ist dabei zu Kontakten mit Personen gekommen, für die er Arbeiten mitgestalten und ausführen sollte. Mittlerweile hat er, beispielsweise, in sieben Kirchen deren Altäre, Fenster und Pulte gestaltet. Als Auftraggeber sind ihm jene mit Handschlagqualität am liebsten. Bei „Verträgen mit tausend Klauseln" seien Schwierigkeiten vorprogrammiert. Unter den Auftragsarbeiten seien drei Kirchen die wichtigsten Projekte, darunter die Millenniumskirche. Künstlerisch seien die „Schwimmenden Steine" das Highlight.

"My works of glass are materialized language."
Rudolf Gritsch

Glass forgives no mistake. Primarily, he works with glass, metal and stone. Materials which "actually don't have anything in common" and are very different. Liquid, transparent, colored, opaque and multifaceted. You have to work with the material, you cannot work against it. With glass "you must comply one hundred percent with its laws, otherwise you get punished." For him it is no coincidence with which material a person works, if it's glass, wood or stone. For him glass is an "alchemical, mystic material" you have to treat with skills, understanding and knowledge in order to combine the shapeable and soft quality as well as the hard and fragile one.

Glas verzeiht keinen Fehler. Vorrangig arbeitet er mit Glas, Metall und Stein. Materialien, die „eigentlich nichts gemeinsam haben" und sehr different sind. Flüssig, transparent, färbig, undurchsichtig und facettenreich. Man muss mit dem Material und kann nicht gegen es arbeiten. Beim Glas „muss man zu hundert Prozent dessen Gesetzen folgen, sonst wird man gestraft". Er halte es für keinen Zufall, mit welchem Material, ob Glas, Holz oder etwa Stein, ein Mensch arbeite. Glas sei für ihn ein „alchemistisches, mystisches Material", dem man mit Können, Verstehen und Wissen begegnen muss, um das Formbare und Weiche sowie Harte und Zerbrechliche verbinden zu können.

top / oben: con-centro / regreso (2010)
On behalf of / Im Auftrag von: Self-commissioned / Eigenauftrag
Kiln-formed, using hand-crafted elements from furnace glass. /
Formengeschmolzenes, klares Ofenglas aus handgeformten Elementen.

bottom / unten: con-centro / verdad (2010)
On behalf of / Im Auftrag von: Property of the artist / Eigenbesitz
Small blown glass balls that are melted together and fused to the top of a volcanic rock. / Geblasene, verschmolzene Glaskügelchen als Basis auf einen Vulkanstein aufgeschmolzen.

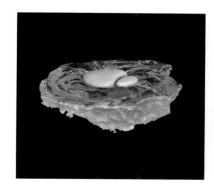

top left / oben links: <u>Floating Stones / amistad</u> (2004)
top right / oben rechts: <u>Floating Stones / equilibrio</u> (2004)
bottom / unten: <u>Floating Stones / punto culmimante</u> (2011)
On behalf of / Im Auftrag von: Glasgalerie Linz
Rocks cannot swim, and yet they can on molten glass. The glass appears
as cooled liquid. / Steine können nicht schwimmen, aber sie können es
doch: auf flüssigem Glas. Das Glas zeigt sich als gekühlte Flüssigkeit.

<u>The inspiring craftsman</u>. Even if he works in an artistic way, he's "always a craftsman". As such he's dependent on tools and he doesn't reject digital technologies. He's tied to computers, microprocessors and 3-D plotters. You have to use today's technologies and in our time you have to "inspire" young people, this is the "elemental force for creating." "I have the skills to do something", you got to be able to say this and to build on that. In teaching he has noticed that "he has to pick up the individual where he is", and that applies for his customers as well.

<u>Der begeisternde Handwerker</u>. Er sei, auch wenn er künstlerisch arbeite, „immer ein Handwerker". Als solcher sei er auf Werkzeug angewiesen und lehne er digitale Technologien nicht ab. Er sei an Computer, Mikroprozessoren und 3D-Plotter gebunden. Man müsse die heutigen Technologien nützen und man müsse in unserer Zeit die jungen Menschen „begeistern", dies sei die „Urkraft für das Schaffen". „Ich kann etwas", das müsse man sagen können und darauf aufbauen. Beim Unterrichten sei ihm aufgefallen, dass er den Menschen „dort abholen muss, wo er ist", was auch für seine Auftraggeber gilt.

The 4-D concept. It is—regarding the 3-D plotter—important to lead life according to the 4-D concept, and that means with "humility, thankfulness, discipline and endurance". "If I look at my own life, if I was successful, much was built upon those four columns." For a craftsman and artist this concept is so important that you have to "question" it over and over again. However, he wouldn't want "to miss any mistake which I have made. I am glad about every mistake." Every mistake has its sense. You learn from every single one. For life.

Das 4D-Konzept. Es sei – in Bezug auf den 3D-Plotter – wichtig, das Leben nach dem 4D-Konzept zu führen, und zwar mit „Demut, Dankbarkeit, Disziplin und Durchhaltevermögen". „Wenn ich mein eigenes Leben betrachte, dann war vieles, falls ich Erfolg hatte, auf diese vier Säulen gebaut." Dieses Konzept sei für einen Handwerker und Künstler so wichtig, dass man es immer von Neuem „hinterfragen" müsse. Er möchte aber „keinen Fehler missen, den ich gemacht habe. Ich bin um jeden Fehler froh." Jeder Fehler hat seinen Sinn. Aus jedem lernt man. Für das Leben.

Rudolf Gritsch

top / oben: Corning Mastervideo IV – kiln-formed glass patternbar trilogy (2002)
bottom / unten: Corning Mastervideo IV – patternbar plate I (2002)
On behalf of / Im Auftrag von: Corning Museum of Glass
These works are part of the "Master Videos" series from Corning Museum, NY.
This film shows step by step how enamel work is produced. / Die Arbeiten sind Teil der Serie „Master Videos" des Corning Museums, NY. In diesem Film wird in Schritten gezeigt, wie Schmelzglasarbeiten entstehen.

Glass / Glas

Blue Wave – Golden Steps / Blaue Welle – Goldene Stiege (2008–2010)
On behalf of / Im Auftrag von: City of Melk / Stadt Melk
Around 2000 blue and gold glass stones guide visitors through the city
to Melk Abbey. / Circa 2000 blaue und goldene Glassteine leiten die
Besucher durch die Stadt zum Stift Melk.

Rudolf Gritsch

Following Water
(2004–2015)

Following Water (2004–2015)
On behalf of / Im Auftrag von: Bullseye Projects Gallery 2015 / 2016
Partly transparent, partly colored glass elements with thick sides. Two structured elements communicate with each other in metaphors about their interaction. / Teils transparente, teils eingefärbte dickwandige Glaselemente. Jeweils zwei strukturierte Elemente kommunizieren in Metaphern über ihre Wechselwirkung zueinander.

„Meine Arbeiten aus Glas
sind materialisierte Sprache."
Rudolf Gritsch

Wilten Abbey, Innsbruck /
Stift Wilten, Innsbruck
(2012)

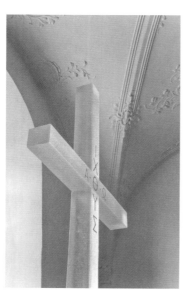

Rudolf Gritsch

Glass decoration of the choir chapel in Wilten Abbey, Innsbruck / Glasgestaltung Chorkapelle im Stift Wilten, Innsbruck (2012) On behalf of / Im Auftrag von: Wilten Abbey / Stift Wilten Made of melted optical glass, the elements are up to 12 cm thick. They were developed with the architectural firm Klaszkleeberger. / Die Elemente sind aus optischem Glas erschmolzen und bis zu 12 cm dick. Entwickelt wurden sie mit dem Büro Klaszkleeberger Architekten.

Rudolf Gritsch   1959 Born / Geb. in St. Pölten • 1976–1979: Apprenticeship in St. Pölten at the Karl Knapp glazier's workshop / Lehre in St. Pölten bei Firma Kunstglaserei Karl Knapp • 1982: Master craftsman exam / Meisterprüfung • 1986: Specialist teacher at the Technical School for Glass Kramsach / Fachlehrer an der Glasfachschule Kramsach • 1989: Started freelance work in his own studio in Kramsach / Beginn der Selbstständigkeit mit eigenem Studio in Kramsach • 1992–1993: Head of development and Artist in Residence at Bullseye Glass Co., Oregon / Leitung der Entwicklungsabteilung und Artist in Residence bei Bullseye Glass Co., Oregon • 2001–2004: Training in drawing and art therapy at MGT Institute in Vienna / Ausbildung in Mal- und Gestaltungstherapie am MGT Institut in Wien • To date / bis dato: Head of the hot glass workshop at HTL Glas und Chemie. Advanced training at the Technical School for Glass Kramsach; freelance work. / Leiter der Heißglaswerkstätte an der HTL Glas & Chemie, Aufbaulehrgang & Kolleg an der Glasfachschule Kramsach; freischaffend.

His entire life is just one glass biography throughout. Glass-blowing. Professional glass school. Glazing craft. Glassworks. With glass the man born in Tyrol wanders the wide world. He gets to Kramsach, Innsbruck and Vienna, to Azerbaijan, Denmark, Germany, England, France, Italy, Czech Republic, the United States of America and back. His own glassworks in Vienna is so to speak the melting pot for the multiple action forces in craft and arts. The large number of exhibitions from Leipzig to Miami are by no means a glass bubble.

Sein ganzes Leben ist eine einzige Glasbiografie. Glasbläserei. Glasfachschule. Glashandwerk. Glashütte. Mit dem Glas kommt der in Tirol geborene in die weite Welt. Nach Kramsach, Innsbruck und Wien, nach Aserbaidschan, Dänemark, Deutschland, England, Frankreich, Italien, Tschechien, in die Vereinigten Staaten von Amerika und zurück. Die eigene Glashütte in Wien ist gleichsam der Schmelzpunkt für die multiplen Tatkräfte in Handwerk und Kunst. Die zahlreichen Ausstellungen von Leipzig bis Miami sind beileibe keine Glasblase.

Robert Comploj

Glass / Glas

Learning in the USA. His career in glass actually starts as a joiner and engineering draftsman. "By chance" and because he wants to do the *Matura* exam, he comes to Kramsach, without knowing "that this has to do with glass". He provided for his own keep first as a joiner, when he "learned" in the United States of America and in England. "In craft, most of it must be understood and cannot be learned. You have to understand glass". First you are not even allowed to touch the glass, "you work towards the goal[1]". "I wanted to master it. That was my first thought." An addiction, in a way.

Lernen in den USA. Seine Karriere in Glas beginnt er eigentlich als Tischler und technischer Zeichner. „Durch Zufall" und weil er die Matura absolvieren will, kommt er nach Kramsach, ohne zu wissen, „dass das mit Glas zu tun hat". Seinen Unterhalt hat er sich zunächst als Tischler finanziert, als er in den Vereinigten Staaten von Amerika und in England „gelernt" hat. „Im Handwerk ist das Meiste zum Verstehen und nicht zum Lernen. Man muss das Glas begreifen." Zuerst dürfe man das Glas gar nicht anfassen, man „arbeitet zu". „Ich wollte es beherrschen. Das war mein erster Gedanke." Sozusagen eine Sucht.

The transparency of glass. "Glass isn't just glass." It's fascinating because it's complex. The cooling, the expansion, the chemicals, the transparency, the melting process, the transparent quality... In a way the glass maker looks like a "clumsy craftsman", actually he is, of course, an artist. As a matter of fact, a scientist, if you think of "the expansion and cooling".

1   By a gradual, step-by-step method, until the final object shape is
    obtained. (Tr. n.)

Die Durchsichtigkeit des Glases. „Das Glas ist nicht einfach Glas." Es sei faszinierend, weil es komplex ist. Das Abkühlen, das Ausdehnen, die Chemikalien, die Durchsichtigkeit, der Schmelzprozess, das Transparente ... Der Glasmacher sehe zwar aus wie ein „plumper Handwerker", in Wahrheit sei er freilich ein Künstler. Eigentlich ein Wissenschaftler, wenn man an „die Ausdehnung und Abkühlung" denke.

Roxy (2015)
On behalf of / Im Auftrag von: Artist's collection / Eigene Kollektion
The surface of the ROXY vase is produced using the centuries old "ballotton" technique (Murano). After each piece cools down, it is elaborately cut and polished by hand. / Die Oberfläche der Vase ROXY entwickelt sich aus einer jahrhundertealten Technik der „Ballotton" (Murano). Jedes Stück wird nach dem Abkühlprozess per Hand noch aufwendig geschnitten und geschliffen.

Worldwide sales. He manufactures everything, from the daily-use glass item to the art object. "We serve many markets." He has a catalog and he makes pots or drinking glasses, also art creations, which he sells worldwide. "A flower pot isn't just a flower pot, but a beautiful object." He receives "special orders" from designers, he makes prototypes. He takes part in fairs in Paris and exports all over the world. "I want to see what is possible with such a tiny company, how I am able to maintain my hold." His objects are also represented by a gallery in the United States.

Weltweiter Umsatz. Er stelle vom Gebrauchsglas bis zum Kunstobjekt alles her. „Wir bedienen viele Märkte." Er habe einen Katalog und stelle Schüsseln oder Trinkgläser her, auch Kunst, die er weltweit verkauft. „Eine Blumenvase ist nicht nur eine Blumenvase, sondern ein schönes Objekt." Er bekomme „Spezialaufträge" von Designern, stelle Prototypen her. Er nehme an Messen in Paris teil und exportiere weltweit. „Ich will sehen, was mit einer so winzigen Firma möglich ist, wie ich mich behaupten kann." Seine Objekte vertrete auch eine Galerie in den Vereinigten Staaten.

"I sell the leaning drinking glasses ten times better than the straight ones."
Robert Comploj

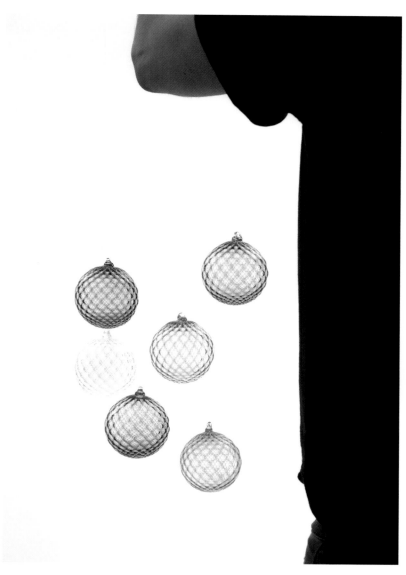

Ornament (2013)
On behalf of / Im Auftrag von: Artist's collection / Eigene Kollektion
Filigree hand-blown balls that can be used individually as a decoration or as Christmas ball ornaments. / Filigrane, mundgeblasene Kugeln, die einzeln als dekoratives Objekt oder als Weihnachtskugeln verwendet werden.

Glass / Glas

Imperfect (2012)
On behalf of / Im Auftrag von: Artist's collection / Eigene Kollektion
Hand-blown water glasses whose shapes are distorted by hand
during the formation process. / Mundgeblasene Wassergläser, die
im Entstehungsprozess von Hand verformt werden.

„Die schiefen Trinkgläser
verkaufe ich zehn Mal
besser als die geraden."
Robert Comploj

Paying dearly for experience. You make your experiences, you pay dearly for that, but you are not supposed to put up with just about everything. "You have to learn that you don't always give in, that you simply take a hard line instead, that's very important. Also as a young business owner." The interaction with customers is a big learning process. The best thing is to write "an order confirmation with all the details". The biggest problem is "the correct calculation" and you just don't learn experience of life at school.

One thousand four hundred glass balls. "Our biggest project was a chandelier for the Red Bull Ring. This was a cool order. A huge project." The lighting fixture was an installation with one thousand four hundred solid glass balls. He made every single one of them himself. Every order is a new challenge. Today he is able to "completely blend" every experience he has made with different customers.

Das Lehrgeld für Erfahrungen. Man mache seine Erfahrungen, zahle Lehrgeld, aber man dürfe sich nicht alles gefallen lassen. „Man muss lernen, dass man nicht immer nachgibt, sondern einfach auf den Tisch haut, das ist ganz wichtig. Auch als Jungunternehmer." Der Umgang mit den Kunden sei ein großer Lernprozess. Am besten sei es, „eine Auftragsbestätigung mit allen Details" zu schreiben. Das größte Problem sei „die richtige Kalkulation" und die Lebenserfahrung erlerne man nicht in der Schule.

Eintausendvierhundert Glaskugeln. „Unser größtes Projekt war ein Kronleuchter für den Red Bull Ring. Das war ein toller Auftrag. Ein Riesenprojekt." Der Leuchter sei eine Installation mit eintausendvierhundert massiven Glaskugeln. Jede einzelne habe er selbst produziert. Jeder Auftrag sei eine neue Herausforderung. Heute könne er jede Erfahrung, die er mit verschiedenen Arbeitgebern gemacht habe, „komplett vermischen".

"Your own handwriting is important". The 3-D printer has no chance to replace him in the near future in the production of glass pots. The people who put his pot in their home are not interested in a faster production, but in "the story behind the item". People don't want "serial products", but individual objects, even with small faults, if they happen. "I sell the leaning drinking glasses ten times better than the straight ones". In any case you shouldn't doubt "about what you do, not even one moment."

„Wichtig ist die eigene Handschrift." Der 3D-Drucker habe auch in absehbarer Zeit keine Chance, ihn bei der Produktion von Glasvasen zu ersetzen. Die Menschen, die seine Vase in ihrem Haus aufstellen würden, interessiere keine schnellere Produktion, sondern „die Geschichte hinter dem Gegenstand". Die Leute wollen keine „Serienprodukte", sondern individuelle Objekte, allenfalls mit kleinen Fehlern. „Die schiefen Trinkgläser verkaufe ich zehn Mal besser als die geraden." Jedenfalls dürfe man an dem, „was man macht, keinen Moment zweifeln".

Foam (2012)
On behalf of / Im Auftrag von: Artist's collection / Eigene Kollektion
The objects are produced from melted-down glass rods that are elaborately polished. The honeycombs that randomly develop are reminiscent of bionic structures. / Die Objekte entstehen aus zusammengeschmolzenen Glasstäben, die aufwändig geschliffen werden. Die zufällig entstehenden Waben erinnern an bionische Strukturen.

Candy Couture (2015)
On behalf of / Im Auftrag von: Artist's collection / Eigene Kollektion
Inspired by Venetian techniques, flower vases were created that have
an effect even without flowers. / Inspiriert von venezianischen Techniken
entstanden Blumenvasen, die auch ohne Blumen als Objekt wirken.

Robert Comploj

Urban Beads (2014)
On behalf of / Im Auftrag von: Artist's collection / Eigene Kollektion
Each element is shaped from a melted-down glass plate into which air is blown.
In the next step, the individual balls are assembled into objects. / Jedes Element
wird aus einer zusammengeschmolzenen Glasplatte geformt und aufgeblasen. Im
nächsten Arbeitsschritt werden die einzelnen Kugeln zu Objekten zusammengefügt.

Robert Comploj   1982 Born / Geb. in Tyrol / Tirol · 2001–2003: Advanced training at the Technical School for Glass Kramsach / Auf-
baulehrgang an der Glasfachschule Kramsach · 2003: Glass studio of Michael Ruh in London / Glass Studio Michael Ruh, London · 2005:
Glassblower at Glas Hagen Hütte in Retschow / Glasbläser in der Glas Hagen Hütte in Retschow · 2006–2012: Glassblower at Kuchlerhaus in
Weigelsdorf / Glasbläser im Kuchlerhaus, Weigelsdorf · 2007: Master class at the Corning Museum of Glass in Corning / Meisterklasse
Corning Museum of Glass, Corning · 2008–2010: Glassblower at Glaspusteri Saeby / Glasbläser in der Glaspusteri Saeby · 2013: Founding of
his own company Glashütte Comploj in Traun / Gründung des eigenen Betriebs Glashütte Comploj in Traun · Since / Seit 2017: New atelier
and gallery in Vienna / Neues Atelier und Galerie in Wien

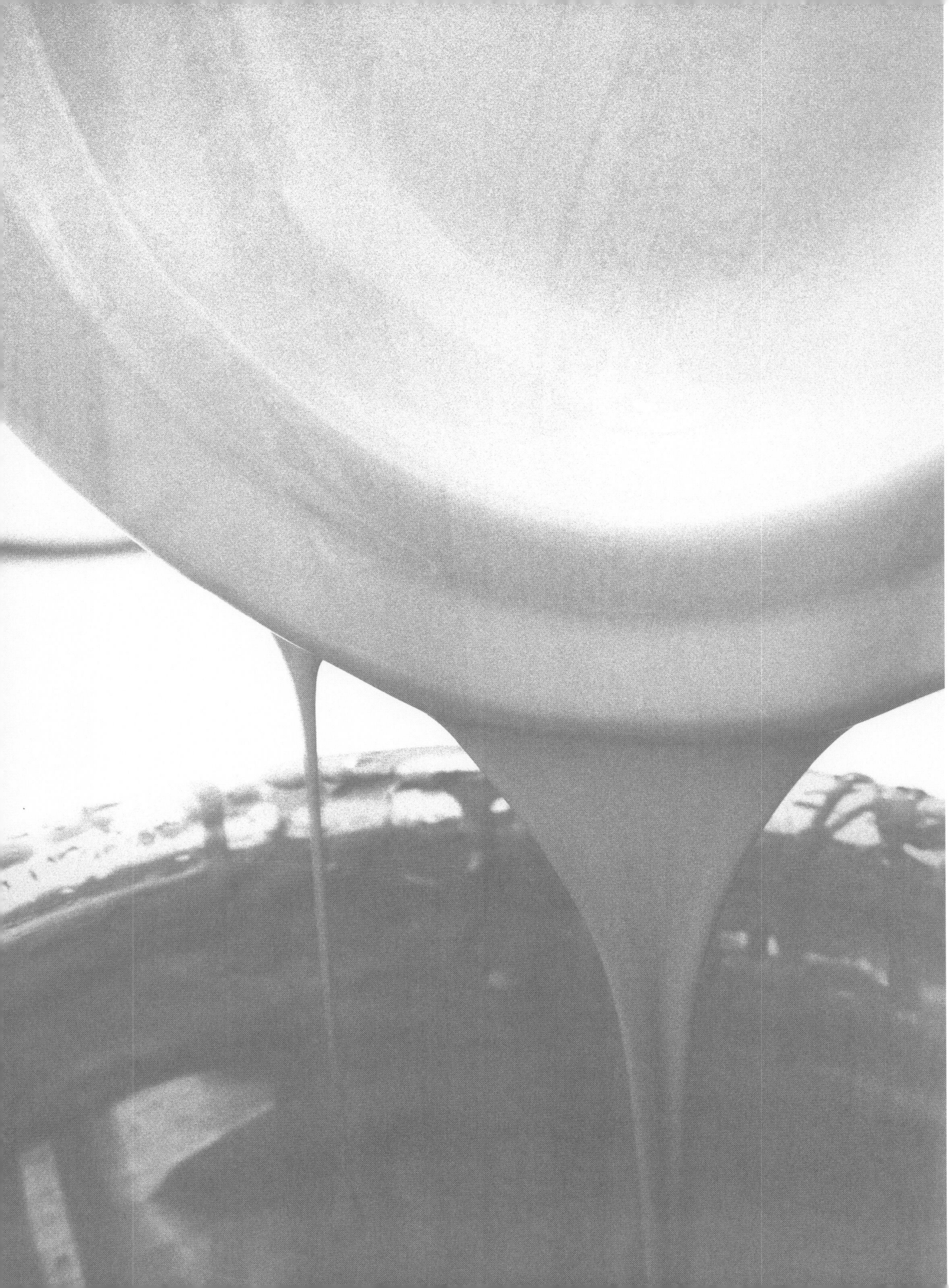

Ceramics is her focus. She became a master in Vienna. At the University of Applied Arts. With Matteo Thun. The glazing took place at the Guildhall University in London. To be precise, at the Department of Furniture and Interior Design. She graduated and was awarded her diploma for her bathroom sink in cooperation with a very well-known company. For three years she was an independent staff member with an architecture bureau in Vienna. Then she founded her own company, with a fine name.

Die Keramik ist ihr Schwerpunkt. Zur Meisterin ist sie in Wien geworden. An der Universität für Angewandte Kunst. Bei Matteo Thun. Die Glasur erfolgte an der Guildhall University in London. Genauer am Department of Furniture and Interior Design. Für ihr Waschbecken in Kooperation mit einer allseits bekannten Firma erlangte sie ihr Diplom. Drei Jahre lang war sie freie Mitarbeiterin in einem Architekturbüro in Wien. Dann gründete sie ihr eigenes Unternehmen mit einem feinen Namen.

Sandra Haischberger

Ceramics / Keramik

Junior high school and People's College[1]. Her "basic understanding" marked by the family was that you can do everything by yourself if "you screw, do, craft." She is an educated *Hauptschule* (secondary/junior high school) teacher. For English and PE. "This isn't going to work out all the way to retirement", she thought, and she started a pottery class at the People's College. Subsequently she went to the University of Applied Arts in Vienna. Majoring in what back then was called Design study. Gastronomic design, ceramics and metal. "It was exactly the right thing." There she also became familiar with porcelain.

1   A nation-wide institution offering adult courses and classes at a low cost; basic, amateur as well as intermediate further education for professional purposes in a very large variety of fields and subjects. (Tr.n.)

Hauptschule und Volkshochschule. Ihr von der Familie geprägtes „Grundverständnis" sei gewesen, man könne alles selbst machen, wenn „man schraubt, tut, werkt". Sie sei ausgebildete Hauptschullehrerin. Für Englisch und Turnen. „Das geht sich nicht aus bis zur Pension", habe sie sich gedacht, und einen Volkshochschulkurs für Töpfern begonnen. In der Folge sei sie an die Universität für Angewandte Kunst in Wien gekommen. Zum damaligen Designstudium. Gastrodesign, Keramik und Metall. „Es war genau das Richtige." Dort habe sie auch das Porzellan kennengelernt.

"Customers have a longing for craft."
Sandra Haischberger

Soldering and welding in London. Before the graduation from university she had been in London for one semester. There she learned soldering and welding. First, she didn't have a real idea about her profession. She "started" in an architecture bureau, "learning quite a big deal" working with upholsterers, joiners and metalworkers. "I am still profiting from that today." She attended a workshop at a porcelain manufacturing company in Hungary and she made a first illuminating light ball in her mini attic, "thirty square meters", "and I didn't want to be standing at Christmas markets all my life".

Löten und schweißen in London. Vor dem Diplom sei sie ein Semester in London gewesen. Da habe sie löten und schweißen gelernt. Zunächst habe sie keine richtige Berufsvorstellung gehabt. Sie habe in einem Architekturbüro „angefangen" und bei der Zusammenarbeit mit Polsterern, Tischlern und Schlossern „irrsinnig viel gelernt. Von dem zehre ich noch." Sie habe einen Workshop in einer Porzellanmanufaktur in Ungarn gemacht und eine erste Leuchtkugel auf ihrem Minidachboden, „dreißig Quadratmeter", hergestellt, „und mein Leben lang auf Weihnachtsmärkten stehen wollte ich nicht".

Atelier sales workshop. "Selling doesn't really suit me." She wants to manufacture, but she doesn't want to sell large quantities by herself. For Laufen[2] she has "made" a free-standing sink, however, she never wanted to be dependent on manufacturers. At the beginning "out of necessity" she "combined" atelier, sales and workshop, in order to realize later that people are fascinated when they watch the production process. People understand that handcrafting, manual work cannot be cheap, but still affordable. However, regarding the number of pieces she's limited.

Exciting prototypes. Now and then she has to reject an order. It would be too costly to develop a prototype for ten pieces and not for one hundred pieces. Nevertheless, sometimes she does accept such orders, because "often it's amazingly exciting stuff."

2   A company for ceramics and stone manufacturing established in 1892, which has its headquarters in Laufen, Switzerland.

Atelierverkaufswerkstatt. „Der Verkauf ist nicht mein Ding." Sie wolle herstellen, aber nicht selber in großen Mengen verkaufen. Für Laufen[1] habe sie ein freistehendes Waschbecken „gemacht", wollte aber nie von Herstellern abhängig sein. Zuerst habe sie „aus Not" Atelier, Verkauf und Werkstatt „kombiniert", um später zu erkennen, dass es die Leute fasziniert, beim Produktionsprozess zuzusehen. Die Menschen verstehen, dass Handarbeit nicht billig sein kann und trotzdem erschwinglich ist. Bei den Stückzahlen sei sie jedoch eingeschränkt.

Spannende Prototypen. Hin und wieder müsse sie einen Auftrag ablehnen. Es wäre zu aufwendig, für zehn und nicht für einhundert Stück einen Prototyp zu entwickeln. Manchmal nehme sie solche Bestellungen dennoch an, weil es „oft irrsinnig spannende Sachen sind".

1   Ein Unternehmen für Keramik- und Steinguterzeugung, das im Jahr 1892 mit Sitz in Laufen, Schweiz, gegründet wurde.

Sandra Haischberger

In the woods... (2014)
On behalf of / Im Auftrag von: Artist's collection / Eigene Kollektion
Large porcelain containers with three different animals that are reminiscent of classic porcelain figurines. For storing biscuits, candy, etc. / Große Porzellandosen mit drei verschiedenen Tierköpfen, die an klassische Porzellanfigurinen erinnern. Zur Aufbewahrung von Keksen, Konfekt etc.

„Die Kunden haben
eine Sehnsucht nach
dem Handwerk."
Sandra Haischberger

Raw. planters (2015)
On behalf of / Im Auftrag von: Artist's collection / Eigene Kollektion
Raw is made of recycled porcelain casting slip from Alice produktion.
The colorfulness cannot be reproduced. Each batch is unique. / Raw
wird aus recycelter Porzellangießmasse der Alice produktion hergestellt.
Die Farbigkeit ist nicht reproduzierbar. Jede Charge ist einmalig.

Ceramics / Keramik

123

Concept determination. If you ask about the actual difference between ceramics and porcelain the principles are defined. "Ceramic is the general term for everything that's burned. Porcelain is a pure artificial product which was invented in China. Basically, three elements are mixed together. Feldspar, china clay and quartz". Marco Polo brought along with him the secret of the "white gold". Every manufacturing factory has its own recipe, that's why some porcelain is whiter, the other one is more creme-colored.

Begriffsbestimmung. Fragt man nach dem eigentlichen Unterschied zwischen Keramik und Porzellan, werden die Prinzipien definiert. „Keramik ist der Überbegriff für alles, was gebrannt ist. Porzellan ist ein reines Kunstprodukt, das in China erfunden wurde. Im Grund werden drei Bestandteile zusammengemischt. Feldspat, Kaolin und Quarz." Marco Polo habe das Geheimnis des „Weißen Golds" mitgebracht. Jede Manufaktur habe eine eigene Rezeptur, weshalb manches Porzellan weißer, das andere cremiger sei.

Sandra Haischberger

Raw (2015)
On behalf of / Im Auftrag von: Artist's collection / Eigene Kollektion
Raw is made of recycled porcelain casting slip from Alice produktion. The colorfulness cannot be reproduced. Each batch is unique. / Raw wird aus recycelter Porzellangießmasse der Alice produktion hergestellt. Die Farbigkeit ist nicht reproduzierbar. Jede Charge ist einmalig.

moonstruck (2005)
On behalf of / Im Auftrag von: Artist's collection / Eigene Kollektion
Porcelain light balls that are perforated by hand while still in a "leather hard" state. / Aus Porzellan gegossene Leuchtkugeln, die in noch „lederhartem" Zustand von Hand perforiert werden.

The meaningfulness of the functional approach. She has always tried a lot. Simply tried. "I think that it's important that you simply do, that you don't let yourself get deterred or intimidated, like 'this has no future, nobody needs that', not a bit of all that." "The function of things is more important to her than the artistic quality. Gold edges are beautiful, but they are not suitable for the dishwasher. "I totally rely on my instinct, that's how I am." Apparently, that's "suitable for everyday life". Durable sustainability-wise.

Das Sinnvolle des Praktischen. Sie habe immer viel probiert. Einfach probiert. „Ich glaube, dass es wichtig ist, dass man einfach tut, sich nicht abschrecken oder einschüchtern lässt, von wegen, das hat keine Zukunft, das braucht kein Mensch." Wichtiger sei ihr die Funktion der Dinge als das Künstlerische. Goldränder seien schön, aber nicht für den Geschirrspüler geeignet. „Bei mir ist es so, dass ich mich total auf mein Bauchgefühl verlasse." Dieses ist offensichtlich „alltagstauglich". Nachhaltigkeitsfest.

Alice – tea & dining
(2013)

Sandra Haischberger

Alice – tea & dining (2013)
On behalf of / Im Auftrag von: Artist's collection / Eigene Kollektion
Hand-cast porcelain service of colored Limoges porcelain. All products are
polished on the outside (bisquit) and glazed on the inside. / Handgegossenes
Porzellanservice aus eingefärbtem Limoges-Porzellan. Alle Produkte sind
an den Außenseiten poliert (bisquit) und an den Innenflächen glasiert.

Sandra Haischberger

Ghost (2012)
On behalf of / Im Auftrag von: Artist's collection / Eigene Kollektion
Each vase has an individual application of real vintage lace. When fired, the thread of the lace burns up without leaving any residue—all that remains is its porcelain coating. / Jede Vase hat eine individuelle Applikation aus echten Vintage-Spitzen. Beim Brand verbrennt das Garn der Spitze rückstandsfrei – zurück bleibt nur ihre Hülle aus Porzellan.

Sandra Haischberger   1969 Born / Geb. in Amstetten · 1993–1999: Studied product design at the University of Applied Arts, Vienna / Studium Produktgestaltung an der Universität für angewandte Kunst, Wien · 1997–1998: Studied Furniture and Interior Design at London Guildhall University / Studium Furniture and Interior Design an der London Guildhall University · 2000–2003: Freelance work for Embacher architectural firm, Vienna / Freie Mitarbeit im Architekturbüro Embacher, Wien · 2005: Founded her own company feinedinge* / Gründung des eigenen Betriebs feinedinge*

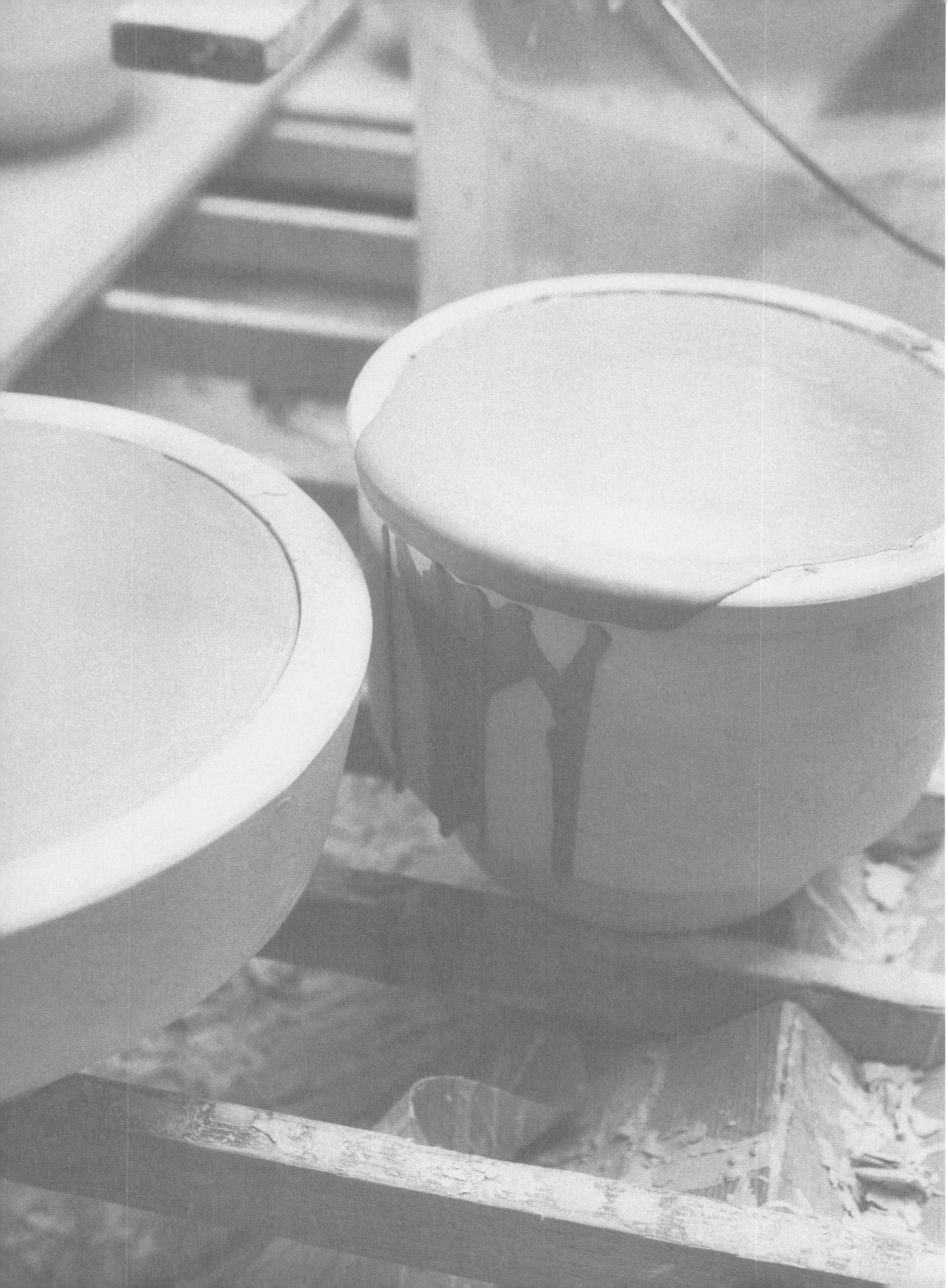

With glass, porcelain and ceramics you can develop many shapes for objects and narrative receptacles. She has learned design not just in Austria. In her skillfulness she also underwent instruction in China, Holland and Japan. Moreover, exhibitions took her to other ends of the world. To China, Korea, Russia and the United States of America. Today you can see her art objects in Graz, Salzburg and Vienna as well as in Milan, San Francisco and Taipei. For example.

Mit Glas und Porzellan und Keramik lassen sich viele Formen für Objekte und narrative Gefäße erarbeiten. Erlernt hat sie die Gestaltung nicht nur in Österreich. In ihrer Kunstfertigkeit hat sie sich auch in China, den Niederlanden und Japan unterweisen lassen. Ausstellungen haben sie ferner an andere Weltenden geführt. Nach China, Korea, Russland und in die Vereinigten Staaten von Amerika. Heute kann man ihre Kunstobjekte in Graz, Salzburg und Wien sowie Mailand, San Francisco und Taipeh sehen. Beispielsweise.

From the home country out to the big wide world. For the manual and artistic skills she was educated in Linz at the University for Arts and Industrial Design. With a diploma. First, she was an employee. One year later she established her own company. With a "one-woman enterprise", that is an atelier in Vienna. To young people today she would suggest "to work on a team". In the first period she taught for two years at a college[1], then for two years she was in the United States and one and a half years in Japan.

1   University-level institution. (Tr. n.)

Aus der Heimat in die große und weite Welt. Für die Hand- und Kunstfertigkeit hat sie in Linz die Universität für künstlerische und industrielle Gestaltung absolviert. Mit Diplom. Zunächst war sie angestellt. Nach einem Jahr hat sie sich selbstständig gemacht. Mit einem „Ein-Frau-Betrieb", das heißt, einem Atelier in Wien. Jungen Leuten würde sie heute raten, „im Team zu arbeiten". In der ersten Zeit hat sie zwei Jahre an einer Hochschule unterrichtet, war dann zweieinhalb Jahre in den Vereinigten Staaten von Amerika und eineinhalb in Japan.

Work from eight to eight. She came to ceramics because she had "the opportunity to go into different workshops and try out different things." She gave a try to textiles "and then, as said, to ceramics". Her notion was that "on ceramics you can live better than on painting". She also liked the material. Her education was not one as a craftswoman that is a manual skills-oriented one, but an artistic one". She had her first atelier in California. "A hovel without electric power and water". Back in Linz she worked "from eight to eight".

Von acht bis acht arbeiten. Zur Keramik sei sie gekommen, weil sie „die Gelegenheit gehabt hat, in verschiedene Werkstätten zu gehen und Dinge auszuprobieren". Sie habe es mit Textil versucht „und dann eben mit Keramik". „Von Keramik", habe sie gedacht, „könne man besser leben als von der Malerei". Auch das Material habe ihr gefallen. Ihre Ausbildung sei keine handwerkliche, sondern eine künstlerische gewesen. Das erste Atelier habe sie in Kalifornien gehabt. „Eine Bruchbude ohne Strom und Wasser." Zurück in Linz, habe sie „von acht bis acht gearbeitet".

"Customers can also be 'cool' and interesting."
Martina Zwölfer

Ribbon vases and heavy metal vases / Bändervase und Heavy Metal-Vasen (2005–2017)
On behalf of / Im Auftrag von: Private / Privat
Hand-shaped rough stoneware clay, cast of fine porcelain, models generated on the computer. Covered with glazes of ash, clay and earth, supersaturated with metals. / Aus grobem Steinzeugton handgeformt, aus feinem Porzellan gegossen, am Computer generierte Modelle – überzogen mit Glasuren aus Asche, Lehm und Erden, mit Metallen übersättigt.

Martina Zwölfer

The uncontrollablility of kiln heat. She works with stone-ware and porcelain. She applies various techniques. She forms by hand, she founds and does pottery. For wood and metal you need tools. "You can manipulate clay almost without any aid. It's soft and malleable." With ceramics "a lot may happen". Once it's inside the kiln you cannot control it anymore at temperatures around one thousand three hundred degrees Celsius, "things may get out of shape or distorted".

The unartistic bureaucracy. "I kind of know everybody and everything." She does different things. Again and again certain receptacle shapes, which she changes just in decoration and shape. She has her favorite cups and mugs. She makes jugs, plates, cups, teapots and

Die Unkontrollierbarkeit der Ofenhitze. Sie arbeite mit Steinzeug und Porzellan. Wende verschiedene Techni-ken an. Sie forme mit der Hand, gieße und töpfere. Für Holz und Metall brauche man Werkzeug. „Ton kann man fast ohne jedes Hilfsmittel bearbeiten. Es ist weich und formbar." Mit Keramik könne „unheimlich viel passieren". Ist es einmal im Ofen, könne man es bei Temperaturen um eintausenddreihundert Grad Celsius nicht mehr kontrollieren, „Dinge können verreißen oder sich verziehen".

Die unkünstlerische Bürokratie. „Ich bin ein bisschen ein Hansdampf in allen Gassen." Sie mache verschiede-ne Dinge. Immer wieder bestimmte Gefäßformen, die sie nur im Dekor und der Figur variiere. Sie habe Lieb-

Viennese jug / Wiener Kanne (2011)
On behalf of / Im Auftrag von: Artist's collection / Eigene Kollektion
The basic form of a triangle standing on its head becomes an eye-catcher through
an unglazed border. Lid anchored in a notch. Teabag held in a slit with a loop. /
Die auf die Spitze gestellte Grundform des Dreiecks wird durch einen unglasierten
Rand zum Blickfang. Mittels einer Kerbe verankerter Deckel sowie ein Schlitz mit
Öse, der Halt für Teebeutel bietet.

Ceramics / Keramik

vases. She has many ideas, but not enough time for executing everything. She has delivered in many countries. Bureaucracy has always asked too much of her, that is why regarding orders a continuity did not happen. She is also unable "to figure out what's economic". She has never made any vases with handles.

Experiences with customers. With customers she has positive and negative experiences. "Cool customers, interesting people" in the meantime have become her friends. She has also been defrauded. "By an Austrian company." She has designed a series of ceramics "without a contract" and has "never seen any money".

lingsbecher. Mache Krüge, Platten, Schalen, Teekannen, Teller und Vasen. Sie habe viele Ideen, aber zu wenig Zeit, um alles auszuführen. Sie habe in viele Länder geliefert. Mit der Bürokratie sei sie immer überfordert gewesen, weshalb bei den Bestellungen keine Kontinuität entstanden sei. Sie sei auch unfähig „durchzurechnen, was ökonomisch sei". Vasen mit Henkeln habe sie dagegen nie gemacht.

Erfahrungen mit Kunden. Mit Kunden habe sie positive und negative Erfahrungen. Mit „klassen Kunden, interessanten Leuten" sei sie mittlerweile befreundet. Sie sei auch betrogen worden. „Von einer österreichischen Firma." Sie habe „ohne Vertrag" eine Serie von Keramiken entworfen und „nie ein Geld gesehen".

Teamwork and machine. "Of course you still keep learning." Above all, you shouldn't do "anything without a contract". Everything is a "long development and design project". Every time you start over from zero. Regarding pots the question is about how to manage that the last drop "doesn't run down" and the handle lies in the hand just "right". She "learned" last for half a year in China. As for her future she would find it appealing "to cooperate with a machine", meaning a 3-D printer.

Teamwork mit Maschine. „Natürlich lernt man immer noch dazu." Vor allem sollte man „nix ohne Vertrag" machen. Es sei alles ein „langes Entwicklungs- und Entwurfsprojekt". Man fange immer wieder bei null an. Bei den Kannen sei die Frage, wie man es anstelle, dass der letzte Tropfen „nicht hinunter rinnt" und der Henkel „geschickt" in der Hand liege. Zuletzt habe sie ein halbes Jahr in China „gelernt". Es reize sie in Zukunft noch, „mit einer Maschine zusammen zu arbeiten", womit sie einen 3D-Drucker meint.

„Kunden können auch ‚klass'
und interessant sein."
Martina Zwölfer

Martina Zwölfer

Wavy dish, soup bowl, rice bowl / Suppenschale, Reisschale (1992–2010) On behalf of / Im Auftrag von: Artist's collection / Eigene Kollektion Bowls and cups thrown on the wheel and plates, pitchers and pots formed of clay slabs. Some with a tenmoku glaze and matte crystalline surface. / Auf der Scheibe gedrehte Schalen und Becher sowie aus Tonplatten geformte Teller, Krüge und Kannen. Teilweise Temmoku- Glasur mit mattkristalliner Oberfläche.

Blossom bowls / Blütenschalen (2003)
On behalf of / Im Auftrag von: Artist's collection / Eigene Kollektion
Elements modeled on petals with one to six notches. Unglazed outside and finely sanded. / Blütenblättern nachempfundene Elemente mit ein bis sechs Kerben. Außen unglasiert und fein geschliffen.

Blossom bowls / Blütenschalen (2003)

Martina Zwölfer

100 Flowers / 100 Blumen (2010)
On behalf of / Im Auftrag von: Artist's collection / Eigene Kollektion
Floral motifs of enamel fired on the bottom that are initially hidden. Limited edition. Made of pure white, translucent Jingdezhen porcelain. / Auf den ersten Blick verborgene Blütenmotive, die mit Emailfarben auf ihre Unterseite aufgebrannt werden. Limitierte Edition. Hergestellt aus weißem Jingdezhen-Porzellan.

Martina Zwölfer   1955 Born / Geb. in Gmünd in Lower Austria / Niederösterreich • 1973–1978: Studied Ceramics at the University of Art and Design Linz / Studium Keramik an der Universität für künstlerische und industrielle Gestaltung Linz • 1980–1981: Studied Ceramics and Glass at Gerrit Rietveld Academie, Amsterdam / Studium Keramik und Glas an der Gerrit Rietveld Academie, Amsterdam • 1990–1991: Studied Ceramics at Kyoto City University of Arts / Studium Keramik an der Kyoto City University of Arts • 1981: Started freelancework / Beginn der Selbstständigkeit

Photo Credits / Bildnachweis

© Adolf Bereuter: p. / S. 70 all / alle
© Albrecht Emanuel Schnabl: p. / S. 64 all / alle
© Beat Buehler: pp. / S. 44, 46
© D. Kvitka (image courtesy of Bullseye Projects): pp. / S. 102 all / alle, 103 all / alle
© Fotostudio Richter in Ebbs: p. / S. 99 top left and right / oben links und rechts
© Fredrik Altinell: p. / S. 90 all / alle
© Georg Kleeberger: p. / S. 104 all / alle
© Hanno Makowitz: pp. / S. 42, 45 center right / mitte rechts
© Inge Prader: p. / S. 41 all / alle
© Jens Lindworsky: pp. / S. 89 all / alle, 92 from top right to bottom left / von oben rechts nach unten links
© Juergen Hammerschmid: p. / S. 57 all / alle
© Katharina Frühwirth: p. / S. 92 top left / oben links
© Martina Zwölfer: p. / S. 135 top / oben, 137 top / oben, 138
© Laura Schreiner: pp. / S. 88
© Meister Eder Linz: pp. / S. 98 all / alle, 99 bottom / unten
© Meusburger: pp. / S. 68 all / alle, 69 all / alle
© Mona Heiß: pp. / S. 80 all / alle, 81 all / alle
© Nikolaus Korab: pp. / S. 9, 19, 20, 21, 22, 23, 24, 25, 26, 27, 28 all / alle, 29 all / alle, 30 all / alle, 31 all / alle, 32 all / alle, 33 all / alle, 34 all / alle, 35, 36, 37, 38, 39, 43 top left / oben links, 47, 48, 49, 50, 51, 60 left / links, 65 all / alle, 66 all / alle, 71, 72, 73, 74, 75, 83, 84, 85, 86, 87, 93, 94, 95, 96, 97, 105, 106 left / links, 108, 109, 117, 118, 119, 120, 121, 129, 130, 131, 132, 133, 134, all / alle, 135 bottom / unten, 136 all / alle, 137 bottom / unten, 139, 143
© Petra Rautenstrauch: pp. / S. 77 all / alle, 78/79
© Rita Newman: p. / S. 91
© Robert Marksteiner: pp. / S. 122, 124, 126 all / alle, 127, 128
© Roswitha Schneider: pp. / S. 59, 61, 62, 63, 67 all / alle
© Rudi Gritsch: pp. / S. 100 all / alle, 101 all / alle
© Simone Andres: p. / S. 125
© Stefan John: p. / S. 58
© Tamara Tinnacher: pp. / S. 76, 82 all / alle
© Tomas Steinert: pp. / S. 52 all / alle, 53, 54 all / alle, 55 all / alle, 56 all / alle
© Vincent Ribbers: pp. / S. 40 all / alle, 43 from top right to bottom left / von oben rechts nach unten links, 45 top right / oben rechts
© Werner Redel: pp. / S. 107, 110 all / alle, 111 all / alle, 112, 113, 114, 115 all / alle, 116
© Wolfgang Zlodej: p. / S. 123 all / alle

Acknowledgements / Danksagung

I would like to express my gratitude to
- Martin Aigner, Peter Bruckner, Robert Comploj, Rudi Gritsch, Sandra Haischberger, Beate von Harten, Arnold Meusburger, Veronika Persché, Thomas Rösler and Martina Zwölfer, whose lives and works provided the basis of this book;
- the author Janko Ferk, who has condensed ten interviews, some of them very extensive, into empathic texts;
- the designer and graphic designer Andreas Pawlik, who has helped develop this publication, and who shares the responsibility for its graphic design with Fanny Arnold;
- the photographer Nikolaus Korab, whose photographs document people, workshops, and projects over the past two years;
- the sociologists Anna Wanka and Julia Pintsuk-Christof, whose meticulous research is the foundation of this book and the basis of further projects;
- my partner Katharina Maria Bruckner and my children Anatol and Cosima for their support!

Mein Dank gilt
- Martin Aigner, Peter Bruckner, Robert Comploj, Rudi Gritsch, Sandra Haischberger, Beate von Harten, Arnold Meusburger, Veronika Persché, Thomas Rösler und Martina Zwölfer, deren Leben und Werk die Grundlage dieser Publikation bildet;
- dem Autor Janko Ferk, der zehn teilweise sehr umfangreiche Interviews zu empathischen Texten verdichtet hat;
- dem Designer und Grafiker Andreas Pawlik, der diese Publikation mitentwickelt hat und gemeinsam mit Fanny Arnold für die grafische Gestaltung verantwortlich zeichnet;
- dem Fotografen Nikolaus Korab, der in den letzten zwei Jahren Menschen, Werkstätten und Projekte fotografisch festgehalten hat;
- den Soziologinnen Anna Wanka und Julia Pintsuk-Christof, deren akribische Forschungsarbeit die Basis für dieses Buch und die Grundlage für weitere Projekte ist;
- meiner Partnerin Katharina Maria Bruckner und meinen Kindern Anatol und Cosima für ihre Unterstützung!

Imprint /
Impressum

Craft-based Design – On Practical Knowledge and
Manual Creativity / Von Handwerkern und Gestaltern

Editor / Herausgeber: Hans Stefan Moritsch

New Design University Privatuniversität GesmbH
Mariazeller Straße 97a
3100 St. Pölten
Austria / Österreich
T +43 2742 / 890 2411, F +43 2742 / 890 2413
office@ndu.ac.at, www.ndu.ac.at

Essays by / Essays von: Janko Ferk
Photos / Fotografien: Nikolaus Korab
Texts by / Texte von: Anna Wanka & Julia Pintsuk-Christof,
Stefan Moritsch
Graphic concept and design / Grafisches Konzept und
Umsetzung: Andreas Pawlik, Fanny Arnold (for / für dform)
Manuscript editing / Redaktion: Stefan Moritsch,
Julia Pintsuk-Christof
English translation / Englische Übersetzung pp. / S. 6–18:
Ada St. Laurent (in other words)
English translation / Englische Übersetzung
pp. / S. 20–134: Michele Bajo
English translation of captions and biographies / Englische
Übersetzung der Bildunterschriften und Biografien: Andrea Kraus
(Übersetzungsbüro Mag. Andrea Kraus)
German proofreading / Lektorat Deutsch: Katharina Ebetshuber,
Mario Jochheim, Andrea Kraus
English proofreading / Lektorat Englisch: Nele Kröger

Paper book block / Papier Buchkern: Focus Art Natural, 135 g
Paper cover / Papier Cover: SH Recycling, 140 g
Print / Druck: Gugler GmbH
Binding / Bindung: Buchbinderei Papyrus GesmbH & Co KG
Typeface / Schrift: Maison Neue, Milieu Grotesque

With a big thank you to our sponsors! /
Mit großem Dank an unsere Sponsoren!

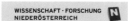

Published by / Erschienen bei
Niggli Verlag, Salenstein
Switzerland / Schweiz
www.niggli.ch

The German National Library lists this publication in the German
National Bibliography; detailed bibliographic data are available on
the internet at http://dnb.dnb.de.

Die Deutsche Nationalbibliothek verzeichnet diese Publikation in
der Deutschen Nationalbibliografie; detaillierte bibliografische Daten
sind im Internet über http://dnb.dnb.de abrufbar.

ISBN 978-3-7212-0979-2

© 2018 Niggli, imprint of / ein Imprint der Braun Publishing AG,
Salenstein, and / und New Design University St.Pölten

1st edition 2018 / 1. Auflage 2018

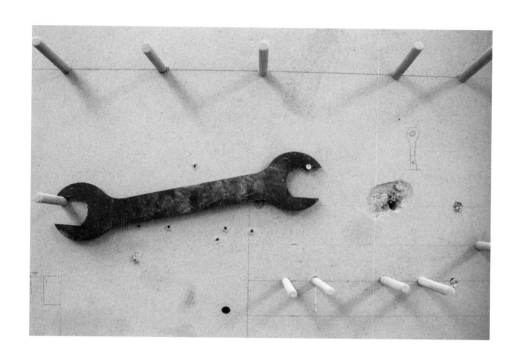